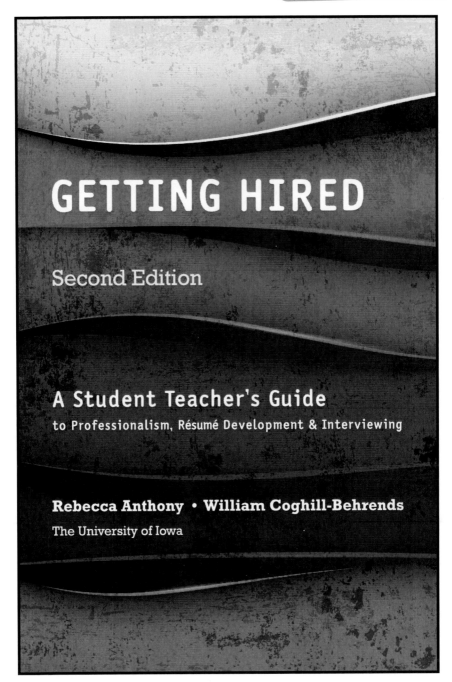

GETTING HIRED

Second Edition

A Student Teacher's Guide
to Professionalism, Résumé Development & Interviewing

Rebecca Anthony • William Coghill-Behrends
The University of Iowa

Book Team

Chairman and Chief Executive Officer   Mark C. Falb
President and Chief Operating Officer   Chad M. Chandlee
Vice President, Higher Education   David L. Tart
Director of Publishing Partnerships   Paul B. Carty
Senior Developmental Coordinator   Angela Willenbring
Vice President, Operations   Timothy J. Beitzel
Project Coordinator   Charmayne McMurray
Permissions Reviewer   Kathy Hanson
Cover Designer   Suzanne Millius
Web Project Editor   Tracy Wiley

Cover and title page image © Shutterstock, Inc.

Kendall Hunt
publishing company
www.kendallhunt.com
Send all inquiries to:
4050 Westmark Drive
Dubuque, IA 52004-1840

Printed in the United States of America
10 9 8 7 6 5 4 3 2 1

Fred and Penny, again we learn from you: Ask the question when it's most opportune. Green doesn't always mean go.

Penny: "It doesn't always have to be fun."

Fred: "Yes, it does."

BRIEF CONTENTS

CONTENTS

PHASE 1   Getting Ready   1

PART 1   The 10 Truths of Student Teaching   3

PART 2   Becoming a Teacher   14

PART 3   The List of 100 Things Employers Will Ask about You   24

PART 4   Ethics and Integrity in the Job Search   33

PART 11   Interview Questions and Topics   125

PART 12   After the Interview   138

ACKNOWLEDGMENTS

The Getting Hired journey started several years ago with a wonderful team. We are excited to continue on the second leg of this journey with the launch of the second edition. First and foremost, thank you, Paul Carty, for loving education and the teachers in your life. We are moved by your belief in the power of education and books like this one to help new teachers find the right job and begin a successful teaching career. It is a pleasure to call you a colleague and friend.

To the second edition team, Angela Willenbring and Renae Wickham: Thanks for helping this project come together.

To the hundreds of teacher leaders who inspire us and, more important, their students every day: Keep it up. You make us very proud.

To Tas and Andy: We treasure your unwavering support and what we learn from you as teachers and social advocates.

Of course, all kinds of people directly and indirectly participated in the creation of this book and in our lives. We appreciate your insight in education: Shane Williams, Andrea Stewart, Jeff McCanna, Mario Andrade, Jake Chung, Diane Campbell, Ross Wilburn, Cindi Duiff, Kristin Rickey, Ann Feldmann, Jim Pedersen, Mary Esdorn, Loren Marvin, Jennifer Barrera, Ashley Smith, Gino Garza, Susan Lagos Lavenz, and Allison Bruhn. We appreciate the insights that you've provided us on life and on being a good teacher: Teri, Hannah, Damond, Quincy, Natalya, Tassie, and Veronica.

PREFACE

In a recent national survey about the teacher workforce of the future, employers indicated they wanted teachers who were passionate about their work, flexible, and good at relationship building. Are you passionate about your work as a teacher? Do you have what it takes to build relationships? Do you know how to be flexible? Chances are, if you're becoming a teacher, you answered yes to each of those questions. In fact, if you've made it this far, you've demonstrated that you have what it takes to be a teacher of the future—and that's important, because never before in the history of the nation has our need for effective teachers been greater. Your important work will help students discover their strengths, will help communities grow, and will help determine our nation's—our world's—future. There are few careers that afford individuals the opportunity and ability to live a life fully, knowing that each day you step in front of a classroom, you are making a difference. You already know that some kids will need a little more from you—a lesson plan revision or accommodation, patience, nurturing. Some will arrive in your classroom ready to learn and others will need your serious attention to take content and make it relevant. They all need your kind heart and your smile. You can do it. And if you're nervous, uncertain, or wondering what it is you'll bring, you're in the right place—we plan to help you figure all of that out, so that when it comes time to get a job, you'll know exactly what to do.

This book is written with one goal in mind: to help you get hired. In order to do that, we first need to help you get ready to make the most of your student teaching experience. In our work with school leaders, we've learned what makes a good student teacher. Even more important, we've learned what good student teachers do to convince employers that they can do the job. Then we'll show you how to get there—to the interview, to the job fair, to the opportunity to seal the deal. You have just one chance when interviewing—one chance to prove to the employer that you are the best candidate. The last phase of the book focuses exclusively on the interview. You'll learn how to make the most of those rare opportunities to wow employers.

This book is organized into three phases. These are: **Getting Ready:** Making the most of student teaching and your work with students; **Getting There:** The job seeking tools and resources of a successful job search; and **Getting Hired:** Nailing the interview—with sound preparation, student-centered thinking, and a firm handshake. We know you'll be very busy during student teaching, so you'll notice that each phase is broken into smaller parts. The parts roughly correspond to the amount of time that most student teachers are engaged in their placement experience (10–16 weeks). Each part introduces an important topic regarding the teacher job search. You'll find valuable information that we've collected from students, cooperating teachers, administrators, and faculty. Their advice adds a level of richness to the text that we think you'll appreciate.

In the end, *Getting Hired* is about your transformation from student teacher to classroom teacher. Your dedication, passion, and true commitment to quality work is what will make you a good teacher. Your stories—the simple things you noticed along the way, how you managed unpredictability and turned that into experience is what will make you a new hire. We need new teachers like you. Let's get hired!

FEATURES OF THIS BOOK

Welcome to *Getting Hired*. The design of this book is intentional. It is not meant to be read from one end to the other without stopping to reflect and complete the activities you'll encounter along the way. The built-in reflective activities and the online ePlanner and Interview Portfolio tools are designed to help you make the most of your experience so you'll be the one to get hired!

TAKE 5

Each part begins with a brief reflection activity to help you organize your thoughts and focus your attention on key experiences and topics to make the most of that particular part. Use these questions to guide your thinking on a particular topic. Some of these questions make excellent discussion points for you with a cooperating teacher, university supervisor, or even your peers. If you truly Take 5, you'll find it easier to answer interview questions and share your beliefs, experiences, and passion for teaching.

TAKE 5 AGAIN

Like the first Take 5, each part has a Take 5 Again—usually a more focused thought and reflection prompt about the materials in that particular part. Take 5 Again activities help turn reflection into action, and thoughts into meaningful interview responses. Don't skip the Take 5 or Take 5 Again—those five minutes here and there end up being powerful interview preparation.

GETTING HIRED WEBSITE

The *Getting Hired* companion website is more than a resource—it's a launchpad for your professional development. On the website you'll find powerful tools to help guide your reflections, student teaching, and job search. You'll also find:

ePlanner Activities

ePlanner activities enable you to really turn student teaching experiences into job seeking stories, your own personal branding, and a professional image that will leave people wondering where you got the insider information. ePlanner activities should be completed at the end of each part—but not forgotten. The ePlanner activities become interview cheatsheets, with valuable information about where you've been, where you are in student teaching, and where you're going.

eJournal

No student teaching experience would be complete without journal reflections that describe your learning, the ups and downs of student teaching, and your realities. These journals are useful in a number of ways and can be used to compare notes and have powerful discussions during your seminars.

Employer Tips

We worked with administrators from across the country to put together the tips and video tips that you'll find throughout the text and on the website. Each video is short and to the point, and each contains a valuable message that you should carry into the next phase of your job search.

eResources

The eResources portion of the website offers valuable job seeking tools from teacher testing and out-of-state licensure to job databases to relocation tools. Utilize the online resources to save you time and energy as you work your way through student teaching and into your first teaching job.

INTERVIEW PORTFOLIO

The Interview Portfolio you'll find in Part 9 of Getting Hired is your all-in-one interview organization, portfolio, web presence, and standards-based teacher tool. You'll find assembling the Interview Portfolio to be a powerful activity as you prepare for your interviews. With step-by-step instructions, directed reflection, and organized sections to clarify your teaching style and experiences, you won't want to go to an interview without one. Not to mention, employers will be impressed with your ability to organize your teaching experiences and learning around the INTASC standards. The Interview Portfolio can be printed as is, attached to an email, or uploaded as a pdf to a website, giving you an ePortfolio tool that will set you apart from the rest when you go on the market. The Interview Portfolio is based on the eight aspects of teaching employers want to know most about.

GETTING HIRED VIDEO

We've assembled short video vignettes that accentuate the details you'll read about in the text. Watch the Getting Hired Videos to get tips from fellow students and employers. In the Getting Hired section, you'll also find three sample interviews: Elementary, Middle/Junior High, and High School candidates provide examples of how to answer the most challenging interview questions. The Getting Hired Videos will launch your job search into high gear and give powerful interview answers to the toughest interview questions. Tune in, and get hired!

ABOUT THE AUTHORS

Rebecca Anthony

Director of Professional Development, Teacher Leader Center, College of Education, The University of Iowa

Rebecca has a long and rich history in career development in addition to her years of professional experience on all sides of the hiring process. Rebecca has been president of the national placement organization, received six major awards, and conducted major research projects related to employment and job search topics. Publications include a number of juried articles, white papers, and journal publications. Additionally she is the co-author of 11 books. Rebecca has presented on topics related to employment issues at national and international conferences. Rebecca, a co-founder of the ePortfolio, has worked with Dr. John Achrazoglou and university colleagues on the development of the ePortfolio, Cyber ToolBox, and Digital BackPack projects since 1996.

William Coghill-Behrends

Associate Director, Professional Development, Teacher Leader Center, College of Education, The University of Iowa

Will has an extensive background in career development, language education, and instructional design and technology. His work and teaching experience span two continents and multiple settings—from elementary schools to college classrooms. He has served on advisory boards for technology and education organizations, and presented at state and national conferences. William has trained hundreds of students and employers on the ePortfolio and works closely with undergraduate and graduate students in the job search process. Will has received a major teaching award at The University of Iowa, currently serves on the UI Executive Board of the Iowa Edge Diversity Project and the leadership team for the Iowa Education Fellows (i-fellows), an initiative to improve the doctoral student experience in the College of Education. He is the author of three books on the job search in Education and Higher Ed.

Rebecca and Will have most recently produced several programs for television about job-seeking topics for academics and have published two books, the *CV Handbook* and the *PhD Handbook,* for use in the academic job search for the graduate student population. Their work has been featured by a prominent state organization and the Governor's Office of the State of Iowa for the professional development of teachers and administrators in the State of Iowa. They are currently spearheading a national survey called "Teachers of the Future," which will examine the needs, nuances, and nature of the 2.8 million K–12 teachers needed in American schools over the next decade.

PHASE 1

Getting Ready

Get ready. Student teaching is your one chance to pull everything that you've learned over the course of your teacher preparation program together. It's your opportunity to try new things, learn as much as you can about schools, students, strategies, and standards. It's your chance to meet parents, paraprofessionals, and principals. It's your one chance to figure out what you believe about teaching and learning and what you know to be true about you as a teacher. Get ready—to change the world.

Chances are you're feeling the nerves. If you haven't already met your cooperating teacher or soon-to-be students, you have to be wondering what they'll be like. They're surely wondering what you're going to be like. It's an exciting event—even for students. Some student teachers become that one person whom the student remembers from their elementary days. Get ready—to build relationships and make memories.

But you probably recognize the steep learning curve that's ahead. You've come a long way, but you know there's a lot to learn. In the next several weeks, you're going to experience so many new situations that will test your ability to stay the course—don't worry, we know you can do it. The first part of this book is devoted to making the most of your student teaching experience, so you don't miss out on anything important or take for granted how fast student teaching will go by. We don't want that to happen to you, so read carefully; employers shared with us their most valuable tips for helping student teachers make the most so they can get hired. Get ready—get ready to have a successful experience student teaching.

This is your chance to become a teacher.

PART 1

The 10 Truths of Student Teaching

"Twenty-first century education is being dramatically redefined through educational reform. We are teaching in new times. These new times require a next generation teacher—what we are calling a teacher leader. We believe that teacher leaders should be at the vanguard of technological applications in the classroom. They should also have a deep and nuanced understanding of assessment practices and understand the role that schools play in building healthy communities."

—Dr. Peter Hlebowitsh, Dean, College of Education, University of Alabama

My To-Do List

1. Discover the 10 Truths of Student Teaching and plan for a successful classroom experience.
2. Set the stage for a productive relationship with your cooperating teacher.
3. Plan for a successful student teaching experience by knowing who you are, finding experiences, not waiting for them to find you, and becoming a strong team player. Be a teacher.

My Project Overview

1. Take 5: Getting Ready for Student Teaching
2. My ePlanner
   a. *Demographics and Data:* Using data to make decisions.
   b. *Field Experiences Summary:* Organize past experiences for future success.
   c. *Goals:* Long and short-term goals to get you ready for your career.
   d. *My Weekly Summary:* Key observations and self-assessment.
3. Take 5 Again: Discover Your Strengths; Know Your Needs

The student teaching experience is a bit like study abroad: total immersion. Those who study abroad are changed by the experience—you too will be changed by student teaching—you'll become a teacher. For some of you this transformation will be very real and noticeable, and for others that change may be less obvious. What's important is to acknowledge and embrace these opportunities for growth as they occur. There is no such thing as a perfect student teacher. You'll enjoy several successes along with a few bumps in the road. All of your experiences during your internship will be beneficial in your development as a career teacher. Employers expect to hear what you've learned during your student teaching, and how those experiences—good and bad—have made you the teacher sitting in front of them at the interview.

TAKE 5

Getting Ready for Student Teaching

It's time to launch the most important part of your development as a teacher. Time to take 5 and write about student teaching. Use the space below to jot down your thoughts about student teaching. Be prepared to discuss these ideas with your cooperating teacher, university supervisor, peers, and a potential employer—you're all part of a team now.

If you were to write a status update on Facebook or Twitter about your first day of student teaching, what would it be (140 characters or less)?

Gandhi once said, "Be the change you wish to see in the world." How do you hope to make a difference as a student teacher?

How would you want students to describe you, the new student teacher, to parents?

IDENTITY IN FLUX

Your student teaching internship is just the beginning of an immense professional identity transformation. Teaching is complicated, and master teachers devote years of attention to the processes, products, and professional knowledge it takes to become a teacher leader. Few careers have such a long development cycle. Teaching is a serious profession, and taking your profession seriously—early on—is a must if you plan to have a successful career in teaching.

Jeff McCanna, Human Resources Director of one of the largest school districts in the nation, says: "Our future rests in our next generation—we must have good teachers in our classrooms. Because of the unprecedented growth in our region, we recruit year-round, in the United States and abroad. Each year we pass school referendums and build new schools—that's the easy part. Finding talented new teachers to help each student succeed is our biggest challenge."

Part of taking your profession seriously means seeing yourself as a professional. Very few student teachers walk into their new classrooms chin up and chest out; in fact, quite the opposite is true. If you're a new student teacher there's a good chance you feel nervous, intimidated, and insecure about your abilities. If that's not enough, some of you are probably even having second thoughts about your chosen vocation. This is totally normal, and in order for us to begin the task of transforming your identity to one that embraces your strengths rather than apologizing for inexperience, we offer 10 truths of student teaching that will inform your job search, and prove to an employer that you have what it takes.

TRUTH #1

You're going to make mistakes—learn from them.

Some may be considered "naturals" in the classroom—but even "naturals" make mistakes. Teaching is a challenge—particularly in 21st century American classrooms. Accept mistakes as learning opportunities. This first transformation will be fundamental in your professional development—not to mention during the interview process. The reflective practitioner is constantly reviewing, observing and taking note of classroom successes and shortcomings. Employers and student teaching supervisors alike will want to hear about your missteps in teaching and—most importantly—how you've turned those mistakes into mastery.

TRUTH #2

Come early, stay late.

Teaching is hard work—and your student teaching experience will demonstrate that this profession isn't for everyone. There will be days where you second guess your ability to stay the course—pay attention to those moments, resolve to work harder. Go the extra mile, put in the extra time—in the end it will pay off not only in an exemplary recommendation, but in the extra knowledge you gained from that hard work. You'll need a good recommendation to get a job and the only way to get that is to prove that you're worth recommending.

❝*We're looking for new teachers who are going to go the extra mile for students and those who truly understand their content knowledge, build relationships with students, and are willing to look at the individual student and their needs—that's what will make a difference in our schools.*❞

—Dr. Mario Andrade, Assistant Superintendent

TRUTH #3

Know your students—know your school.

Unfortunately too few student teachers really get to know their students in the short period of time that they spend in the classroom. This isn't necessarily a time issue—it's an issue of initiative. Employers need individuals who are able to make a connection to the students in their classrooms. You know from your teacher education coursework that American classrooms are composed of diverse learners who bring all sorts of variables to the learning environment. How can you possibly be an effective teacher without knowing your students? A concerted effort should be made to know the demographics of the community, school, your classroom, in addition to the unique learning needs of individual students. Perhaps your school or community has unique alternative programming or resources available to families. Each school is different, and a thorough examination of your field experiences will reveal the different contexts in which you've already worked. How were your field experiences similar? How were they different? How can you describe the various student populations you've experienced during your studies? Employers are curious about how well you've gotten to know your students and thus how committed you are to the success of all learners.

TRUTH #4

When working with adults—act like an adult.

Teaching is high stakes in this day and age. That means your cooperating teachers, teacher preparation program, and university supervisor have a lot riding on you. They're going to need to give you feedback and sometimes even take corrective measures to ensure that your experience—and the experience of your students—is what it should be. Most of you will waltz through student teaching with no conflict—but few of you will leave with no disagreements. They might be small disagreements—you might teach something or approach something differently—or they might be larger in scale—you completely disagree with how a discipline situation was handled, or you felt embarrassed with the way your cooperating teacher called you out when you did something wrong. It's never easy to address potential conflicts that may arise between student teachers and cooperating teachers, but it is realistic to acknowledge conflict and address it when it occurs. Most difficult conflicts are the result of avoidance and inattention to improve. Often, student teachers take offense to honest feedback they receive from cooperating teachers, supervisors, even the students. Feedback is a good learning tool—listen to it, learn from it, and don't take it personally. Most conflict is easily rectified in the form of utilizing different approaches, reconsidering a lesson plan, or making creative changes to the learning environment. Seldom is conflict so severe that individuals beyond the student teacher/cooperating teacher team need to be involved. Conflict during your student teaching is a good dose of reality for work in the real world. Conflict is a normal part of worklife—and conflict resolution is a critical skill—and one that employers want to hear you address.

TIP

Dr. Kristen Rickey, Superintendent, suggests that serious thought be put into how you have handled an adult disagreement in a school setting. "If you can't talk about a difference of opinion or style, then I might assume that you won't be able to handle a conflict when one does arise. Good conflict resolution skills are important for students and teachers."

TRUTH #5

Practice makes perfect—organize, plan, practice.

The need to be organized as a teacher goes without saying, but we're going to say it again: Organization is key—and essential to running an effective classroom as well as an effective job search. Teachers are constantly thinking on their feet—but teaching isn't spur of the moment. It's thoughtful, deliberate, and intentional. Planning is imperative as is practice (and we really do mean practicing everything from delivering your instruction, to introducing yourself to new colleagues or parents). You'll be able to make the most of your student teaching by staying organized, and developing a clear plan for your experience that addresses your responsibilities, teaching time, planning time, and opportunities to reflect on your experience. By having a clear plan for your placement, you'll make better use of your time. Don't forget, most of you will also be in the midst of the job search. Plan ahead, practice often, and utilize all organizational tools possible at your disposal, including those in the ePlanner.

TRUTH #6

Be a collaborator and team builder—get to know your partners in teaching and learn from them.

Your cooperating teacher and university supervisor are but two of the individuals who make up your student teaching team. From faculty members and fellow student teachers to para-educators and even parents—there are so many individuals involved in the school enterprise that it's almost impossible to know where a working relationship begins and where one ends. It's critical that you understand how you as a student teacher and future teacher will fit into that web to maximize the effectiveness of your own collaborations, and most of all to promote student success.

You!

TRUTH #7

Time is not on your side—learn to prioritize early.

Establishing priorities is never easy—particularly when you're not exactly sure what your responsibilities or expectations will be. One approach is to establish a list of goals or things you hope to accomplish during your student teaching. Certainly some priority setting will occur naturally as you become more familiar with your students, your schedule, and the setting.

TRUTH #8

Prove it or lose it.

In a standards-based profession like teaching, you're going to have to demonstrate professional skills. An employer will need proof that you're able to meet the demands of the classroom while delivering a grade A instructional product. Your student teaching experience is designed so that you'll gain experience with all the inner workings of a classroom in your particular content area. An elementary classroom teacher works in a different context than a secondary foreign language teacher. You'll need to address your context by knowing the needs, realities, and outcomes of your particular area. You'll also need to have experiences with classroom management, providing accomodations and differentiated instruction for various learners, family involvment, assessment, lesson planning, communication, professional development, and competence in understanding the culture and environment in which learning occurs. There are a number of ways to demonstrate these competencies—from portfolios to the strategic way in which you'll answer interview questions. The best start is to notice everything and be incredibly attentive to your intention to make the most of this experience.

TIP

"During your student teaching experience, you will meet master teachers, who are savvy professionals. These are also the folks who wind up on interview teams. They aren't necessarily looking for a ready made master teacher—they are looking for someone who has what it takes to become a master teacher. Prove that you can do it!"

—Shane Williams, Director of Elementary Innovation & Instruction

TRUTH #9

Know who you are.

This knowledge will serve you well as it helps you identify your needs, and make the most of your strengths. Every student teacher should enter their classroom knowing exactly what needs they have and what strengths they can immediately put to good use. A great deal of self-help literature focuses on improving that which we can't do well. It is our opinion that a much better approach to addressing weaknesses is to focus instead on what you can do well. You can count on sharing your special attributes, your best abilities, and your exceptional qualities with potential employers. Start by listing a strength that you now have. (*Odds are good that it will be adjusted by the time you are finished with student teaching.*) These simple statements will help you eliminate the uncomfortable hesitation when you are asked to talk about your strengths and possibly a weakness, too.

TAKE 5 **AGAIN**

Discover Your Strengths, Know Your Needs

Time to take 5 more minutes and discover your strengths and know your needs. Chances are you'll be asked to talk about it. Use the space below to jot down your thoughts about student teaching. Be prepared to discuss these ideas with your cooperating teacher, university supervisor, peers, and of course, a potential employer. They'll want to know what you have to offer.

If students could give your past field experiences (or other related work) a grade— what aspects of your work with them would get an A?

What aspects of your work with students in past experiences would get a C or below?

TIP

Start talking about your weaknesses as "areas of growth," "needs," "or skills in which you wish to improve."

That alone will help you transform weaknesses into experiences.

Use your weakness to set an attainable goal for student teaching—one that is realistic and will be of benefit to you as you search for jobs. For example, take a look at the table below of common perceived weaknesses of student teachers:

PERCEIVED WEAKNESS	PROPOSED GOALS
Classroom discipline	• work with challenging students, • implement behavior support mechanisms, • develop own classroom discipline philosophy.
Experience with parents/families	• send parent newsletter, • create classroom blog, • participate in parent teacher conferences.
Differentiating instruction	• observe special learning programs, • examine Individual Education Plans, • adapt lesson plans for multiple groups.

Having a plan to address your perceived weakness will make your experience more meaningful, and it gives you useful information to discuss in an interview. Notice that each of the weaknesses were written in the form of needs statements. We find this approach makes addressing your shortcomings as a new teacher more practical. The general goal statements that follow each need are attainable, reasonable, and believable.

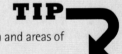

TIP

Let your cooperating teacher know what you hope to accomplish and areas of growth for your student teaching. They can't read your mind!

TRUTH #10

Student teaching is the beginning of the job search— you are a professional.

Yep, the college days are over; from the moment you step into your student teaching classroom you are a professional. You might not feel like one, and unfortunately, students old enough to know the difference between you and your cooperating teacher will do their best to give you a run for your money. From day one, you have a big stake in how you and your work are perceived by the students, teachers, administrators, supervisors . . . all those people that make up the web of your classroom. Nerves are requisite and may even be of benefit, if you turn that initial nervousness into positive energy and motivation to get involved from day one.

TIP

"Initiative is very important."

- "When I'm walking down the hallway, is the student teacher greeting students?"
- "When I walk into the classroom, is everything ready?"
- "Is this student teacher seeking opportunities to meet people, to interact with the students?"
- "Is this student teacher looking for every opportunity to learn?"
- "I want to see dedication, serious planning, and intentional actions in a student teacher."

—Evelyn Cosmos Smith, Assistant Principal

SUMMARY

The 10 Truths of Student Teaching

Now that you've learned about the 10 Truths of Student Teaching you'll be able to make the most of your experience. If you've already started student teaching, don't sweat it—you can incorporate the ideas from the 10 truths starting right now. Treat each day of student teaching as a new start, a new challenge, and a new opportunity to grow as a teacher.

ON THE WEB

Make the most of your student teaching placement and get ready to get hired. These activities will help.

ePlanner Activities

1. *Demographics and Data:* Using data to inform decisions.
2. *Field Experiences Summary:* Organize past experiences for future success.
3. *Goals:* Long and short-term goals to get you ready for your career.
4. *My Weekly Summary:* Key observations and self assessment.

eJournal

1. Write your thoughts about each of the 10 Truths of Student Teaching. Better yet—provide specific examples of actions you've taken or plan to take to make each truth a reality. Employers will likely ask you about each of these truths.
2. Conflict resolution is an important skill for all adults but especially teachers who are responsible to so many different constituents. Write about a conflict you've encountered with another adult in a professional setting (nothing personal here). What was the situation? What did you do to resolve it? And what did you learn as a result? Employers want to know that you'll be a productive and professional colleague.

Video Tips

Making the Most of Student Teaching: listen up as an administrator shares his advice for making the most of student teaching. He'll share how you can be in the top 10 percent of job seeking candidates who won't have to worry about finding a job.

PART 2

Becoming a Teacher

66*It's important that prospective teachers demonstrate an ability to build relationships across their community. I want to see evidence that they have engaged people from diverse backgrounds in a meaningful way, through volunteer or service learning experiences. I also want them to strengthen their real-world knowledge by showing that they can engage a school community and work with students and families facing real problems.* 99

—Dr. Peter Hlebowitsh, Dean, College of Education, University of Alabama

My To-Do List

1. Learn about and integrate the personality and professional traits of effective teachers.
2. Get dressed to impress your students, supervisors and potential employers.
3. Dive into your discipline, examine your beliefs, and communicate your content.

My Project Overview

1. Take 5: Transitioning from College Student to Classroom Teacher
2. My ePlanner
   a. *My Content Area:* Pedagogy, content, and ways of knowing in my field.
   b. *Top Issues:* Know the critical issues facing education and your field.
   c. *My Book List:* Professional materials that make me better.
   d. *My Weekly Summary:* A quick and easy recap of the week.
3. Take 5 Again: Building Relationships and Making a Difference

Your student teaching will form the basis of your professional identity as you actively seek employment as a teacher. Few fields require so many competencies—from content knowledge to pedagogy, knowledge of developmental stages to classroom management, not to mention teaching strategies, teaching standards, and teaching styles—it's a lot to keep track of. In fact, you might find the entire process a bit daunting, but don't fret, because we're pretty convinced that successful student teachers do four important things during student teaching. Do these four things and you'll have a very successful experience:

- Become a professional
- Build relationships
- Teach your content well
- Examine your beliefs

Did we mention that these four things will also prepare you well for your teacher job search? Yep, administrators are looking for someone who is professional, can teach kids well, knows why they want to teach, and who knows how to build relationships. In this part you'll learn about ways to make the most of your student teaching to invigorate your job search.

TAKE 5

Transitioning from College Student to Classroom Teacher

It's time to really think about who you are now and who you'll be after student teaching. For most of you, the end of student teaching also signifies the end of college life. Can you really just be a few short weeks away from the end of the "best years of your life"? Yep. Sorry. But teaching can and will be an amazing adventure too. Let's take a minute (or 5) to write about this important transition.

What do you find most daunting about finishing student teaching and graduating from college?

What was the pivotal event that made you decide to become a teacher and enter your teacher preparation program? Employers almost always ask a question similar to this—be prepared to share.

In what ways will your wardrobe change during student teaching and as a teaching professional?

If you could add any article of clothing to your professional wardrobe, what would it be?

BECOMING A PROFESSIONAL

Easier said than done, right? Wrong! Being a professional is as easy or as difficult as you make it. Here's why. When it comes to professionalism, there are only two key characteristics to perfect: look and act like a teacher. You're not a student anymore (really). If you've made it far enough to student teach, everyone thinks you're professional and capable, including your college professors, university supervisors, cooperating teachers, parents (of the kids you're teaching), and building administrators! Sometimes the last one to get the "You're a professional now" memo are the student teachers themselves! And um, sorry, your parents generally won't think you're a professional until you're off their payroll.

Looking the Part

So it's time to lay those flip flops to rest, and put the baggy sweat pants away until Friday night at 5 (and yeah, you might think you'll be going out on Friday still, but wait until your first Friday of student teaching arrives—90 percent of you will be asleep earlier than the kids you taught!). Yep, you need to dive into that far corner of the closet . . . the one that contains your "dress clothes," and haul them out, because you're about to begin professional boot camp.

Look clean and put together. You don't want to distract anyone, kids included, with your clothing or unprofessional attire. Those teaching at the secondary level should place particular importance on professional attire to distinguish oneself as a professional and establish a professional and productive working relationship early on. High school kids can be pretty brutal if you haven't earned their respect. Not to mention the incredible boost in self-confidence you're likely to give yourself by checking out the new "professional" you in the mirror on your way out the door. You look great.

> **❝**You should be warm and welcoming to students and dress in a professional manner. You are not going clubbing. You might want to be trendy in your dress but please don't be provocative—act and dress like a professional. How you dress and how you carry yourself say a lot about your character.**❞**
>
> —Dr. Mario Andrade, Assistant Superintendent

Acting the Part

How does a teacher act anyway? We could really have fun with stereotypes . . . the flighty foreign language teacher, the laid back art teacher, and the frantic elementary teacher, but we'd likely offend lots of people and perhaps we already have. Acting like a teacher means exhibiting a few key behaviors that will be critical to your success . . . but more importantly, critical to the success of the students in your classroom.

Some rules of thumb:

1. You're the adult. Remember that.
2. Make it clear that you care about the content: how students learn it, and how you teach it.
3. It's OK to say no, in fact, you should get good at it.

EMPLOYERS CARE ABOUT IT!

About your professional demeanor and that includes how you look. Your student teaching experience should be treated like a really, really, really long interview. People are watching you and noticing:

- Your clean appearance
- Your trimmed nails
- Kempt hairstyles
- Ironed tops and bottoms (yep—gotta get out the iron 'cause pulling clothes from your floor won't work!)
- Professional yet comfortable shoes (those little ones keep you on your toes)
- Body art covered, make-up shouldn't look like art
- Piercings and jewelry kept to a minimum
- Well trimmed facial hair
- Attentive and interested posture

Go back to the top of the list—do you care about it?

BUILDING RELATIONSHIPS

It's not as hard as it sounds and if you're going into teaching, you're probably a natural at it. But if not, and if you've got the jitters about making a good impression on your cooperating teacher, future employer, and others who have a stake in your professional outcomes, here's something to remember. Building relationships in a professional setting involves a great deal of interpersonal skill, but it all really boils down to one simple idea—strive to show you care, strive to make a difference by doing your best. If you strive to do those two things regularly in your relationships with students, cooperating teachers, colleagues, peers, you'll definitely be a successful relationship builder. Be prepared to talk about the strategies you used to form and maintain relationships with:

- Students
- Parents
- University supervisors, faculty,
-    and staff supports
- Teachers
- Administrators
- Volunteers
- Administrative staff
- School staff
- Community members

You'll need to articulate your ability to work well with many individuals when you go on the market. Interview questions and behavioral inventories or assessments often revolve around your interactions with various stakeholders in the educational process. Remember the 10 truths of student teaching? Many of those dealt with building relationships—from knowing your students to classroom management to navigating work-related conflict—each of you should be able to speak definitively about your skill in building relationships. Building relationships starts with you.

TAKE 5 **AGAIN**

Building Relationships and Making a Difference

The best teachers all have one thing in common—they know how to build effective and productive relationships with all involved in the educational process: students, parents, colleagues, administrators, community members. They are bridge builders, collaborators and effective listeners. They care to make a difference and know that to make a difference hinges on relationship skills. Brainstorm ways you can demonstrate your skill at building relationships with the following individuals. Provide examples for each based on your experience. If you don't have an experience with a particular group—seek one out, or recognize it as an area of growth. Employers are eager to find out ways you'll be a bridge builder in their district.

Students:

- With disabilities:
- With challenging behavior:
- With exceptional talents:
- With language barriers (non-native speakers, speech and/or language delay):

Cooperating Teachers/School Staff:

Building Administrators:

University Supports (supervisor, faculty, career office):

TEACH YOUR CONTENT WELL

Student teaching is the most important part of your teacher education program because it gives you the opportunity to truly embrace your identity as an emerging teacher. Just think about all you learned about teaching during your practicum and previous field experiences—now multiply that by about a thousand and you'll arrive at what we hope is the amount of learning that will take place during your student teaching experience. This is your chance to really figure out who you are. Focus on what you already know: your knowledge of how kids learn, your content knowledge, and your passion. That's a powerful potion for great teaching. Employers want to hear about your content knowledge and how you plan to share that with your students, how to motivate them to learn your content, and how to make it accessible to all learners.

In the secondary areas like math, science, world languages, or social studies, individuals who make up a department may have vastly different skill sets and experiences that make them uniquely qualified to teach in their area. A German teacher might not be able to waltz into an Honors Advanced AP Calculus class and just begin teaching as easily as they'd be able to teach the conjugations of the verb "to be" in the simple past tense (although for most of us it would be hieroglyphics either way). In elementary classrooms there is often a more common background knowledge and experience base that candidates bring to the classroom. Hopefully, over the course of your field experiences, you've been able to identify your strengths and potential weaknesses with respect to your content knowledge.

My Content Knowledge and Knowledge of the Field

As licensed practitioners in either a secondary area or elementary education, you'll be responsible for being the expert in your field. That means knowing all there is to know about the content you'll teach, but also the most effective ways to teach that content. Elementary teachers, like their secondary peers, are required to demonstrate mastery of content and pedagogical knowledge. Additionally, elementary teachers are required to demonstrate their mastery of the *multiple* components of an elementary curriculum. But that's not all. Your standards-based identity also means that you'll be familiar with your profession. Start by taking an inventory of what you know about your field.

You'll need to communicate a thorough knowledge of your field and demonstrate that you'll be a connected and well informed teacher in your particular discipline. You need to know everything you possibly can about how to be a _____ teacher. (Fill in the blank with your content area). All teachers have to know:

- Developmental stages and how these intersect with content learning in the core areas;
- Key concepts in school readiness, issues in school reform, poverty's effects on schools, approaches to delivering instruction at the various levels;
- The knowledge base and population characteristics of their students.

See where we're going with this? If you're able to communicate all those things to an employer, there'll be no stopping you on the job market. If you think you need to work on any of those skills before you enter the market—now's your chance. To some extent potential employees can ascertain this information on the basis of test scores, coursework, and portfolio examples, not to mention the kinds of experiences you'll write about on your résumé. Remember, writing about it is one thing, but you'll need to be able to talk about it too.

Student teaching gives you an opportunity to organize and reflect on your abilities, experiences, and motivation in a way that your coursework can't. Have you taken the time to consider what makes you an effective teacher? What qualities do you have as a student teacher to help students achieve success? Do you see yourself as a professional, strive to build relationships, and know your content and how to deliver it? If you struggle to answer those questions—you've just created a student teaching to-do list. Endeavor to gather specific experiences so that you can articulate and demonstrate your identity as a teacher.

EXAMINING MY BELIEFS

Over the next several weeks of your student teaching experience you'll develop a better understanding of your own philosophy of teaching and learning. Your philosophy of teaching and learning forms the backbone of your job search. It informs how you describe yourself, it guides your search for an employer, and it helps you to find the right fit. It is critical that you learn to identify and articulate your philosophy, because you'll need a core set of principles to guide your interview answers. Your core philosophy will guide everything, from the way you structure your learning environment to the manner in which you interact with others—from students to parents to colleagues. Chances are you've already had to formulate a philosophy statement in your methods coursework—perhaps even to enroll in your teacher education program.

❝The best philosophy statements are those that tell me what you believe, why you teach, and how you teach. Your teaching philosophy—and the way you integrate this philosophy in your classroom—can determine the difference you make in students' lives.❞

—Ann Feldmann, Assistant Superintendent

Your task now is to see if your lofty vision for teaching and learning measures up, is transformed, and matures over the course of your student teaching semester.

Employers too, will want to hear about your philosophy of teaching and learning. They'll also ask for concrete evidence and specific examples that reflect your philosophy statement. In particular, employers are interested in how your philosophy of teaching meets and reflects the school's mission. They're looking for a real understanding of the process of instruction, and a deep understanding of the various ways students learn. It's more than that, though . . . a philosophy statement includes:

- *Why* we want to be teachers and educate students;
- *What* education means to us, and what it is;
- *How* education occurs: the methods, approaches, and mantras of teaching that guide our work with students.

Take the worry out of writing your philosophy statement and use the three-point check-off scheme to put together a meaningful statement that you own.

A QUICK AND EASY THREE-POINT CHECK-OFF SCHEME FOR WRITING A PHILOSOPHY STATEMENT

☑ **# 1. Why**
Why do you want to be a teacher?
Why are you called to this profession?

☑ **# 2. What**
What does education mean to you?
What are the goals of education?
What does your classroom look like?

☑ **# 3. How**
How do you teach kids?
How do you reach kids where they are?
How do you plan to make a difference?

Because you have written the story in your own voice using authentic examples, feel empowered to share it with others.

Educators routinely revisit their philosophy for reasons both personal and professional. Your philosophy statement will likely be strengthened by your student teaching. Examining your teaching behaviors and reflecting on your beliefs will promote positive change and personal growth. Let your vision grow during student teaching by revisiting and reflecting on your teaching philosophy frequently.

A vision helps one stay focused and committed to a purpose. In essence, your philosophy is your vision.

SUMMARY

Becoming a Teacher

Making the transition from college student to career professional is no small task. From remaking your wardrobe to remodeling your identity, there's a lot to think about. Make it an even more effective transition by completing the activities on the next page.

ON THE WEB

ePlanner Activities

1. *My Content Area:* Pedagogy, content, and ways of knowing in my field.
2. *Top Issues:* Know the critical issues facing education and your field.
3. *My Book List:* Professional materials that make me better.
4. *My Weekly Summary:* A quick and easy recap of the week.

eJournal

1. Write your thoughts about your relationship-building skills. Provide specific examples of how you demonstrated flexibility, a collaborative spirit, and open-mindedness during student teaching.
2. Why do you want to be a teacher? Include specific examples that helped you determine this career path, and experiences in student teaching and other field experiences that helped affirm your choice to become a teacher. Write down two beliefs about teaching and learning you would include in a philosophy statement.

Video Tips

A Student's Perspective of Winning Job Search Strategies: Feeling overwhelmed with student teaching? You're not alone. Listen in as a student teacher on the market reflects on her experience and offers sound advice to use student teaching as a launch pad for the rest of your career.

PART 3

The List of 100 Things Employers Will Ask about You

Dr. Kristen Rickey, Superintendent, advises: "Take your field experiences seriously. All of my interview questions will be about them. Use this opportunity to get as much experience as you can—not only in your classroom but in the entire building. We want candidates who understand how the whole system works to help kids learn."

My To-Do List

1. Develop your road map for student teaching: figuring out what you can do and what you have yet to do.
2. Translate student teaching experiences into interview answers.
3. Establish clear goals for student teaching.

My Project Overview

1. Take 5: The Final Countdown
2. My ePlanner
   a. *My Goals Revisited:* Review your goals from the beginning of student teaching.
   b. *My Weekly Summary:* A week in review promises a better next week.
3. Take 5 Again: Your Roadmap for Career Success

Employers from all occupational fields are routinely surveyed by organizations that collect data about what they find most valuable in new hires. Not surprisingly, many survey results point to *evidence of a successful internship experience.* Why do employers rate this higher than teamwork, communication skills, coursework, or grades? Perhaps it is because your internship reflects all of the other components. It's hard to be successful in a school-based setting without demonstrating teamwork, without speaking clearly, or without using the knowledge you have gained in coursework. An internship can give the employer a sneak preview into how well prepared you are to enter a classroom setting of your own. So far we've talked about the personality characteristics that make teachers successful, the necessity to develop a standards-based teaching identity, and your teaching philosophy. It's now time to bring all of that together—as you will during the student teaching experience—for quick review so that you can move onto some serious job seeking.

TAKE 5

The Final Countdown

Sometimes student teaching suddenly sneaks up on you. You've been busy with coursework and field experiences, not to mention your free time as a college student. Student teaching arrives and your world is turned upside down. You're living, breathing, and dreaming about your placement. Sometimes, students get so wrapped up in student teaching (which is a good thing) that they forget that the job search, or "the Real World" as your folks might put it, is close at hand. This chapter is all about the 100 or so things you have to experience before you leave the test grounds. Employers will have lots of questions for you soon—now's your chance, it's the final countdown. Take 5 minutes to answer the following questions.

What's one technology you really hope to use in your own classroom? What is the benefit for students?

Think about your best lesson plan to date. Why was it effective? What did you enjoy about it? What did the students enjoy?

If you could press the rewind button on a past classroom management situation, which situation would it be and how would you edit it?

As you review the following list of 100 things employers will ask about you, be keenly aware of your current placement in student teaching. Chances are you're still at the beginning of your experience—a good time to take stock of all the experiences you'll need to address with an employer during the interview process.

THE LIST OF 100 THINGS EMPLOYERS WILL ASK YOU

So we present to you a list of 100 things, to do's, must see's, and have to's for student teaching. This is your last chance to pull together some incredibly rich experiences to share with an employer. You'll find out in a later chapter that the competition for the best teaching jobs is fierce—if you're able to relate your 100 experiences to an administrator, chances are you'll be signing a contract!

Collaborations

Did you have any experiences working with the following individuals:

1. Special education teachers and support staff
2. Teaching team in a core subject area like math, science, or language arts
3. The specials team, including:
    a. Fine arts (music, art)
    b. Physical education/health and wellness instructors
    c. Home economics instructors
    d. Keyboarding/computer science instructors
    e. Industrial technologies (woodworking, automotive, design courses)
4. Parents
5. Behavior specialists
6. Guidance counselors
7. School psychologists
8. School social workers
9. Speech-language pathologists
10. Administrators

Accommodations and Differentiated Instruction

Did you have experiences providing accommodations for, or differentiating instruction for learners in any of these situations?

11. Non-native speakers of English, or English language learners
12. Newly immigrated (urban, international)
13. Vision disabilities
14. Hearing disabilities
15. Reading disabilities
16. Math/computational disabilities
17. Behavior disabilities
18. Writing disabilities
19. Intellectual disabilities
20. Social and emotional disabilities

Instructional Strategies and Lesson Planning

Did you have experiences planning lessons and developing materials related to these areas?

21. Assessing student needs
22. Pacing
23. Multiple intelligences
24. Instructional strategies
25. Motivation
26. Content relevance and connections
27. Prior and background knowledge
28. Content knowledge
29. Instructional delivery/methodology
30. Assessment (formal and informal)

Technology

Did you have experiences with the following technologies, or do you have the necessary knowledge and ability to teach effective use of these technologies?

31. Interactive white boards (such as SMART and Promethean Boards and Tables)
32. Tablet devices (such as iPads and eReaders)
33. Smart phones and cell phones in the classroom
34. Internet research and safety for students
35. Assistive technologies
36. Apps and web-based tools for learning
37. Simulations (3-D mapping, virtual reality)
38. Distance education, teaching online
39. Video creation, editing, design, and sharing tools
40. Social media and social learning (Facebook, MOOCs)

Classroom Management

Did you have experiences managing the behaviors of individuals and groups?

41. Proactive management strategies: PBIS
42. Specific management strategies or programs
43. Consequences and student discipline
44. Culture of behavior at the school
45. Classroom management framework/expectations
46. Self-esteem and confidence-building
47. Attention/relevance/connections
48. Motivation and management
49. Reinforcing positive behaviors
50. Parent communication

Assessment

Did you assess student learning both informally and formally?

51. Instruments
52. Philosophy of grading, standards-based grading
53. Formative evaluation
54. Summative evaluation
55. Needs assessments
56. Daily assessments (informal assessment)
57. Diagnostic testing
58. Reporting
59. Standardized testing
60. Methods of assessment (alternatives to assessment)

Core Curriculum and Content Knowledge

Did you use professional standards in your lesson planning, in your self-evaluation, in your professional conversations?

61. State teaching standards, including the Common Core
62. Professional teaching standards
63. Content area standards
    a. Math
    b. Science
    c. Foreign language
    d. English
    e. Social studies
    f. Music
    g. Art
    h. Technology
    i. Physical education/health and wellness
64. Content-specific teaching methods
65. Project-based learning
66. Trends in content area
67. Debates/controversy in content area

Professional Identity/Development

Did you learn, reevaluate, or alter the following things?

68. Teaching philosophy
69. Conflict-resolution skills
70. Career plans (short-term, long-term)
71. Short- and long-term learning goals
72. Teaching strengths and special abilities

73. Technology integration skills
74. Specialized training
75. Certificates/Licensure
76. Passion
77. Extracurricular

Learning Environment and Classroom Culture

Did you implement effective policies, operations, and strategies in the following areas?

78. Homework
79. Classroom layout/blueprint
80. Classroom environment
81. Classroom-based action research (response to intervention)
82. Resources
    a. Print
    b. Technology
83. Home communication
84. Parent/family involvement
85. School functions
86. Typical day
87. Professional Learning Communities (PLC)

Issues in American Schools Today

Did you gain experience or heightened awareness of the following issues in schools?

88. Poverty
89. Mobile populations
90. Diversity and cultural awareness
91. NCLB and Common Core standards
92. Crisis issues
93. Dropout/retention
94. Bullying/cyber bullying
95. Global awareness
96. Readiness for learning
97. Mental health/health and wellness
98. At-risk behaviors
99. Civility/ethics/values
100. Sustainability and environmental issues

TIP

Engage in meaningful conversations with your cooperating teacher and other staff members.

Consider them a knowledge-bank, and take as many withdrawals as you can!

The goal of your student teaching internship is to expose you to the multiplicities present in school classrooms. It would be too simplistic to ask you to cross off each item on the list once you've had a singular experience with that particular item. Take homework, for example; what are the potential connections this essential piece has to poverty and parent and family involvement?

How does homework relate to the "culture of learning" of the particular school? Some schools have homework policies or mandates—from none to a bit from each class. Your future school may be vastly different from your current placement, but the experiences you're gathering now will inform that later position. Employers will expect the big picture with little details.

Your preparation wouldn't be complete without putting everything together one last time—big and small, simple and complex; be prepared to talk about it all.

In the end, the candidates who do best during an interview are those who have attended to the meticulous details of their student teaching placement. They've been keen observers, immediately recognizing their shortcomings or areas where they're lacking in experience, and have sought to fill those gaps with meaningful opportunities. You may not be able to cross all 100 items off your list, but it is our hope that you've taken the message to heart. Some student teachers will find themselves working with cooperating teachers and administrators who ensure that student teachers receive good mentoring and deep learning experiences. Others of you may be in situations where you'll need to be more proactive and attentive to your needs by actively seeking opportunities to gain more experiences from the "list of 100."

TAKE 5 **AGAIN**

Your Road Map for Career Success

It's time to haul out your atlases and calibrate your GPS for student teaching: You need to develop a road map for student teaching. But before you do that, let's figure out where you're going. Take 5 minutes to think about the questions below:

As you reviewed the "List of 100 Things . . ." what experiences are missing from your background?

Are there any shortcuts you can take to get experience quickly or to better prepare yourself to talk about these issues with employers?

This list is daunting, and the journey will be long. What are you doing to unwind after you leave your student teaching placement site?

SUMMARY

The List of 100 Things Employers Will Ask about You

As a student teacher, you have only a short time to gain the rich experiences and broad range of "talking points" necessary to convince employers that you have what it takes to make a difference for students. Our list of 100 things employers will ask about you is a call to arms of sorts, a wake-up call, an action list of items, experiences, individuals, and students you should be able to talk about with an employer. Make your 100 things . . . an integrated part of your student teaching experience by completing the suggested activities that follow.

ON THE WEB

ePlanner Activities

1. *My Goals Revisited:* Review your goals from the beginning of student teaching.
2. *My Weekly Summary:* A week in review promises a better next week.

eResources

Visit Education Week (*www.edweek.org*) and peruse the headlines for the top stories in Education for that particular week. Do any of them relate to your particular experience? How? Education Week is a tremendous resource for staying up-to-date on K–12 related news and headlines.

eJournal

1. You've probably already spent some time in your student teaching placement. Take an item from the list of 100 and write about it. Describe the experience, and how it will benefit you in your next teaching position. Employers are curious about your areas of growth.
2. In which of the areas from the "List of 100 . . ." does your cooperating teacher seem to have the strongest skill? How do you plan to incorporate the observed talents of your cooperating teacher into your own classroom?

PART 4

Ethics and Integrity in the Job Search

Ross Wilburn, Equity Director and Central Office Administrator, gives this advice: "Job seekers need to be careful with résumé enhancement or overselling your background or experience during the interview. Chances are there is someone at the table who knows someone you know or one of your references knows individuals at your school!"

My To-Do List

1. Understand the importance of ethics and integrity in the teaching profession.
2. Proof your job search materials for information accuracy—an employer will.
3. Review state and federal employment laws and your rights during the job search.

My Project Overview

1. Take 5: Pinocchio's Job Search
2. My ePlanner
   a. *Application Draft:* Application accuracy and preparation.
   b. *My Weekly Summary:* A quick and easy recap of the week, because it's a good idea.
3. Take 5 Again: Ethics in Assessment

Truthfulness and accuracy are so important in the job search that they need their own space. Honesty and accuracy apply to every stage and every step of the job search. What you say, what details you include on an application form, how you describe a relevant experience or events in the past—all matter to employers. According to a number of employers, an alarming increase in "applicant fraud" is occurring. In fact, a large human resource professional association reported that employers regularly uncover mistruths about length of employment, salaries, former titles, degrees, and grade point averages. Get your job search started right, by getting your facts right—the first time around.

Accuracy about academic degrees and experiences is critical. Even the slightest discrepancy can be damaging.

TAKE 5

Pinocchio's Job Search

Most of you are probably familiar with the story of Pinocchio. If not, here it is: Pinocchio was a wooden puppet who desperately wanted to become a "real boy." Through some fairy tale magic, he's given the opportunity to turn into a boy provided he can be honest. This seems to be a challenge for Pinocchio and to make the point clear to the audience, his nose grows longer every time he "embellishes" the truth. We want to make sure that your nose isn't growing during the job search. Employers are paying attention. Someone always "Nose" the truth. Take 5 and answer the following questions:

Everyone has at least one blemish, maybe a poor grade from a college class; maybe you got into some trouble during high school or college. Take a moment to think about what you learned from the situation. Then move on!

Students look up to their teachers with much admiration. List three simple things you'll do to ensure you're seen as an ethical, honest, and respectable individual.

TIP

Employers and the courts take fraud very seriously. Protect yourself and your career by telling the truth.

The discovery of inaccuracies, untruths, or misrepresentation will usually preclude further consideration of your candidacy. Once hired, the discovery that you have provided false information can be cause for termination. Most school districts have developed a written policy so that their district does not become a victim of applicant fraud. The wording may vary from district to district, but generally they remind the applicant that any misstatements and/or omissions about the applicant's background or education are grounds for dismissal whenever discovered. The clause "whenever discovered" is an important one. A person could be well into their teaching year and be dismissed on the spot for a falsification on an application form or a résumé. Obviously, this situation would make future job searches difficult as well.

School districts protect themselves from negligent hiring by documenting efforts to verify the background of candidates. Employers routinely conduct employment and background checks to avoid liability in case an unfortunate situation should arise. As a future teacher, you can now see why fingerprinting is required, and why criminal background checks and child abuse registries are carefully reviewed by human resource officials.

If you're making application in a different state, make sure you completely familiarize yourself with the requirements for employment in that state. You may be required to submit fingerprints, background check information, and proof of your eligibility to work in the United States. The following list summarizes some of the procedures used in verifying employment applications and records. State and federal agencies take employment practices seriously. *So should you!*

Verification Procedures

School districts are mandated to verify the following:

- official transcript
- signed application form
- fingerprints
- certification in subject area
- criminal background check
- child abuse registry
- proof of eligibility to work in the United States
- references from past experiences

Employers are required to verify, verify, verify. Candidates need to check, double check, and even triple check. Even a simple mistake in reporting your grade point average, terms of employment, or graduation date—even if done unintentionally—can be interpreted as a misrepresentation. It's not the employer's job to catch your mistakes. It is their job to make sure they're hiring the best, brightest, and most qualified individual. A simple typo, while relatively innocent, can have big implications for your job search goals.

EMPLOYMENT LAWS

While you don't need to research any of the following employment laws, job seekers need to understand that many laws are on the books to protect their privacy and to keep the employer out of legal trouble. Here's a partial list of employment laws. As you can tell from the name of the laws, nearly every aspect of employment and personal rights and privacy issues are regulated by the law. We'll get into more detail about pre-employment inquires and inappropriate interview questions later.

STATE AND FEDERAL EMPLOYMENT LAWS
Laws exist for the protection of the individual and the employer

Title VII of Civil Rights Act of 1964

Civil Rights Act of 1991

Family and Medical Leave Act of 1993

Americans with Disabilities Act of 1990 (ADA)

Equal Pay Act of 1973

Age Discrimination in Employment Act (ADEA)

Rehabilitation Act of 1973

Pregnancy Discrimination Act of 1978—Fair Labor Standards Act (FLSA)

Immigration Reform and Control Act of 1986 (IRCA)

Illegal Immigration Reform and Immigration Responsibility Act of 1996 (IRAIRA)

Older Workers Benefit Protection Act of 1990

National Labor Relations Act (NLRA)

Employee Polygraph Protection Act of 1988

Occupational Safety and Health Act (OSHA)

Consolidated Omnibus Budget Reconciliation Act (COBRA)

Health Insurance Portability and Accountability Act of 1996 (HIPAA)

Drug-Free Workplace Act of 1998

Veterans Re-employment Rights Act

Employee Retirement Income Security Act of 1974 (ERISA)

Fair Credit Reporting Act (FCRA)

Fair Labor Standards Act

Executive Order 11246

42 U.S.C. Section 1981

TRUTHFULNESS MATTERS

There are two primary areas where the truthfulness of candidates is called into question. The first would be exaggeration or embellishment of experiences, namely overstating your role in a particular environment or initiative. Some students, in an effort to demonstrate experience working in diverse settings, might exaggerate the racial or ethnic diversity of a particular school or classroom. Employers work closely together on a variety of initiatives, so most are well aware of the schools and communities in a given area. Not to mention, it just sounds phony when someone isn't being exactly honest during an interview or on a résumé.

Another common mistake candidates make is failure to list criminal convictions or citations when asked for this information on an application. We understand why—they're embarrassing, often not a big deal in the grand scheme of things, and we feel like they reflect on our character. Hey, everyone is allowed a mistake or two in life. Besides, employers were college students once too—they know the routine and they know what you were doing last Saturday night. They did it too! Several of you may have alcohol or moving vehicle violations. Most misdemeanors won't bar you from employment. Failure to list them will! These sorts of infractions always turn up on a criminal background check—so be prepared to talk about how that misstep turned into a learning experience.

Occasionally, applications will state something like: *List all criminal convictions and citations. Do not list moving vehicle violations.* A conviction or deferred judgment related to driving under the influence of alcohol (DUI, OWI) is not considered a moving vehicle violation—even though you may have been driving. Come on, let's be honest, you knew this! Everyone makes mistakes—even big ones sometimes. Employers will still consider you for the job—but only if you're honest, and only if you're able to talk about how you learned from your experiences.

Employers and employees alike are protected by laws that deal with just about every employment or pre-employment circumstance. Employers have to be able to demonstrate why one candidate was hired over another—that's why they check documents—even check them twice. If they catch you being anything but honest, sorry Charlie, you better keep sending applications out, because you just lost a job. So remember, be you, be honest, be real. In the end, it's the only thing you can honestly sell.

❝*If you have a criminal conviction on record, just list it. Whether it's an alcohol-related offense or some other silly mistake from your past, tell us up front. These things don't automatically disqualify you from consideration, but if you fail to list these convictions and we discover them—which we always do—I'm not allowed to consider you any further. You'll be permanently removed from our list of qualified candidates. Be honest. If you're not, you're going to have a hard time finding a district to work for.*❞

—Jeff McCanna, Human Resources Director

TAKE 5 **AGAIN**

Ethics in Assessment

There are a multitude of high stakes decisions riding on student assessment these days. There are a number of issues related to ethics and integrity in assessment itself—what are the goals of the assessment, what decisions do you make based on outcomes, and how will that affect students—even small measures can have a big impact. How do you remain ethical and ensure that your assessment procedures are ethical, fair, and balanced? Can you think of a situation where these issues might be problematic in your own experience?

SUMMARY

Ethics and Integrity in the Job Search

Teachers are held to a high standard of integrity—it makes sense; we want our teachers to model the highest level of professional and ethical behavior for our children and community. The following activities are available to help you get organized and verify that your employment and application materials are absolutely accurate.

ON THE WEB

ePlanner Activities

1. *Application Draft:* Application accuracy and preparation.
2. *My Weekly Summary:* A quick and easy recap of the week, because it's a good idea.

eJournal

1. Spend some time this week recalling an event from your past that you are less than proud of. If you have a criminal offense or some other sort of infraction that may be revealed during the application process, write about what happened (dates, offense, results) and then focus on what you learned from the situation. How were you transformed by that opportunity? Sometimes the greatest adversity presents the biggest opportunity.

2. If a student were to receive a failing grade in one of your classes and you knew that the student would face serious consequences as a result of their not passing your class, like not graduating, dropping out of an extracurricular, or missing an important event, would you still assign a failing grade to the student?

PART 5

Professional Web Presence

Ann Feldmann, Assistant Superintendent, shares this information with job seekers: "It's not uncommon for us to Google candidates. It's not uncommon for us to login to Facebook and Twitter. Most candidates are aware that we are looking at them. They seem to be cleaning up many of their sites. What you have to remember, though, is to ask your friends to clean up, too. If your friends have pics of you, if they have stories about you, we'll see them, too. As hiring officials, we are concerned about your image—for the sake of our students, our district, and our community."

My To-Do List

1. Google yourself to locate information about you on the web.
2. Give your Facebook a professional facelift, by checking for inappropriate content.
3. Learn whether you're Net (or Not) worthy of a job: professional presence in the dirty digital age.
4. Create a separate professional Facebook, Twitter, and/or LinkedIn account.

My Project Overview

1. Take 5: Facebook, Twitter, Pinterest, Oh My
2. My ePlanner
   a. *My Weekly Summary:* Because the week wouldn't be complete without one.
3. Take 5 Again: Are You Net or Not Savvy?

The Internet has transformed our lives in immeasurable ways. From information access to the sharing of knowledge, it's undeniable that an enormous paradigm shift in education is occurring that will completely remake the way we live our lives, much as the introduction of the automobile restructured our society in the early 20th century. You have grown up in a period of time very different from that of most of your college professors and cooperating teachers. You've grown up online! From online scrapbooks your parents have put together to the multiple social networks and file sharing platforms—there's a lot about you out there! In this part, we'll look at the information out there about us, because we know that employers are. Nothing can derail a job search faster than bad information about you on the Internet.

TAKE 5

Facebook, Twitter, Pinterest, Oh My

One question we always ask when doing job search seminars is how many people in attendance have a Facebook or Twitter account, or participate in social networking. Everyone raises their hands—even the most unlikely of individuals. Take 5 minutes to think about the following questions:

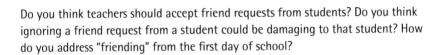

Let's say Facebook's privacy settings were hacked and everything was available to everyone. Would you be kicked out of your placement?

Do you think teachers should accept friend requests from students? Do you think ignoring a friend request from a student could be damaging to that student? How do you address "friending" from the first day of school?

Have you ever searched for students, faculty, or others on the web? On Facebook? On Twitter? What are you looking for?

❝We always Google new candidates—it gives us a sense of what they've been up to before coming to our district and is a good indication whether they'll be a asset or a liability. We need employees who understand the importance of clear boundaries, professionalism, and responsible behavior.❞

—Dr. Jake Chung, Principal

KNOW YOUR DIGITAL FOOTPRINTS

Digital footprints are traces of us online. Our digital footprints include online social media sites, memberships in organizations, work and university related information, photos, blogs, news releases, and articles. The fact is that most are surprised at the amount of information available. This is particularly true of more recent college graduates and those whose graduations are fast approaching. You live, work, and play online—you do everything on the Internet these days, from banking to submitting homework assignments, to paying bills, to socializing. The Internet is the place to be—and as a result, we leave all kinds of traces of our actions out there in cyberspace. We like to avoid gross overgeneralization, but it's probably true that most individuals reading this book have participated in online socializing (come on, raise your hands, how many of you are on Facebook?). Time to take stock of what's out there about us. Time to become digital detectives and do a little "sole" searching because you need to know where your digital footprints lead.

In a conversation with a school administrator who had just finished searching for a new staff member, this was shared:

> **"**We will reject candidates because of social media site content. The candidate was by far the favorite of the interview team but lost the job because of his blatant indiscretion in cyberspace. That said, please, future teachers—know that your professional reputation is to be protected and that employers definitely Google, Twitter, Facebook, etc. As a search team, we have found SERIOUSLY questionable Facebook content (sexual content, alcohol, etc.) for teacher candidates. I hope I don't sound hopelessly traditional—I am only 36.**"**

—Cindi Diouf, Administrator

TIP

Google yourself on the Internet. View the top 100–200 entries about yourself. Trust us—your employers, students, and even some parents are checking you out!

We're not anti-Facebook—we are pro job. You don't want to throw your first job opportunity away because of a picture of you on the beach last summer enjoying more than the water and sun! We hope you've had a lot of fun in college—that's what college is for, but now it's time to turn your attention toward your future. It's important for you to know now, because we don't want your student teaching experience to go awry because a parent, student, or cooperating teacher brought some interesting photos, blog posts, or comments to your principal's attention.

A FACEBOOK FAIRY TALE

The Three Little P's of Facebook . . .

(No, we're not talking pigs!)

You'd be surprised how many people have Facebook pages these days—even your students will want to friend you. Like the little pig who was wise enough to build a house of brick, and not let the wolf in, we too, think there are some folks that you just shouldn't let into your social networking site . . . it can really blow your career away.

Here are our three P's of Facebook:

- Parents
- Pupils
- Professionals in your school

Never friend these folks! You might get asked and it might be awkward, but don't give in—just change the subject.

Also don't:

- Make posts or comments about your student teaching—tacky!
- Let people tag photos of you . . . especially the one from last weekend!
- Let people make inappropriate comments on your wall—Delete!
- Allow anyone who's not a trusted friend to access your profile.
- Use Facebook to network with recruiters you meet. Just because they're on Facebook, doesn't mean they use it for work!

But What If I Can't Get off Facebook?

Even though we want you to be careful of mixing your personal and professional identities on Facebook, plenty of teachers use Facebook in their classrooms by creating groups or pages. So rather than being you on Facebook, you might be "Biology Honors at Anytown High." Facebook pages are preferred over groups, because as page administrator you can post, but not necessarily as yourself. Your activity appears as the name of the Facebook site—keeping you in control. There are dozens of professional resources online about using social media. We suggest ISTE (the International Society for Technology in Education); www.iste.org is a great place to learn about how to incorporate Facebook, Twitter, and other social media in your instruction in a safe and engaging way.

Some new teachers find it difficult, particularly at the secondary level, to establish clear boundaries with students. They're usually not that far apart from you in age, and let's face it—you want to be liked and it's fun to socialize online. At the elementary level some students may already participate in social networking, though at this level it's more likely you'll encounter friend requests from parents or others in your building. This intermingling of personal and professional life opens the door for misinterpretation and conflict. It's so easy for online behavior to be taken out of context. Socializing with students over social networks is a serious no-no. In fact we encourage you to avoid becoming friends online with anyone at your student teaching site and in your future teaching position—that includes students, parents, teachers, coworkers and administrators. Too many new teachers have gotten into serious trouble—even lost their jobs or been removed—for online behavior. You're bound by a strict code of ethics, confidentiality, and professionalism. Mixing work and play is a dangerous combination.

While it is important for you to build relationships with students—even relate to them in a way that they connect with—it's never a good idea to have poor boundaries. Even after the student teaching experience, make sure you maintain a professional relationship—and sometimes that means distance from students. If you're confused about those boundaries, be sure to talk to a cooperating teacher or university supervisor. They can likely provide you with some good strategies to help maintain professional relationships. As a teacher—even student teacher, you're going to be held to a higher (dare we say) "moral" standard. Here's a good motto as you figure all this out: Log out.

❝*Keep your private and professional social media separate. I'm constantly watching for the latest update on my professional Twitter. I have learned so much using these media professionally—new teachers can, too. Social media use helps you stay connected and get the latest on new developments in education, informs your practice, gets your voice out in the community, and is globalizing education. I encourage new educators to develop a professional online presence and to give their students practice doing the same.*❞

—Andrea Stewart, Teacher, Innovator, Competency-based Education Specialist

Offer other ways for students to connect with you outside of the school day should they have questions—an email address, class website, or before- or after-school office hours—are great ways to show your interest and make yourself available to busy students. This communicates a sincere interest in building relationships, but also establishes clear professional boundaries.

TAKE 5 **AGAIN**

Are You Net or Not Savvy?

In the amount of time it has taken to read this chapter—there's a good chance something about you was just transmitted through cyberspace—an email, comment from a friend on Facebookor a tweet!

Here's our quick list for a web-savvy and safe job search.

Google yourself—view the top 100–200 results. How many pertain to you?

Are there photos of you out there?   ☐ yes   ☐ no

Google close friends and family members who might also post or have posted information about you. How many did you Google?

Don't accept friend requests from students, teachers, and parents. How will you reply if you are asked outright about becoming friends over Facebook?

If inappropriate information exists, be ready to talk about it, should it come up.
Topics:

Utilize an ePortfolio to ensure that there's positive and, more importantly, professional information about you.
URL:

SUMMARY

Professional Web Presence

The digital age is upon us and has changed our lives in profound ways. Indeed, our classrooms and manner of teaching are undergoing major transformation. The technology skills the next generation of teachers brings to the classroom will pave the way for this transformation—and guess what—as a digital native, you're in the driver's seat. But be sure to fasten your seatbelt—in other words, take precautions like adhering to professional ethics and codes of conduct involving your online activities. The employment police (your supervisors, future administrators, and faculty) are paying close attention to you and are also on that same information superhighway.

ON THE WEB

ePlanner Activities

1. *My Weekly Summary:* Because the week wouldn't be complete without one.

eJournal

1. Every district and school has developed a "Technology Plan." If you were to deliver a technology plan for you and your classroom, what would it look like? What kinds of technologies would you use, and why?

PHASE 2

Getting There
Landing the Interview

You're probably already a few weeks into your student teaching experience and beginning to feel the effects of working with kids for eight or more hours straight a day. Most of you are having a great time, interacting with students, building relationships, becoming teachers. Some of you are feeling overwhelmed with this chosen vocation, your school, the burdens and repetitive nature of classroom management . . . it's beginning to feel a little like you're on repeat. Each day the same thing, the grind, the wear of the commute. Buck up. You're looking for a job. College was fun while it lasted but, like all good things, it too must end (unless you become a career student—the great thing about teaching is that you can do just that).

You've slowly grown accustomed to getting up five hours earlier than usual. You can make it through an entire day of work not feeling like you're about to fall over from exhaustion at any minute. You now totally understand why most teachers drink coffee and, better yet, the allure of energy drinks. Those students sure gave you a run for your money at first, but now that they've gotten to know you, they're beginning to settle down. The students have tuned into your body language and know what your raised eyebrow means. Yep, you're on your way to becoming a teacher.

You begin to realize some things about yourself as a student: college life pretty much rocks. A few hours of classes every day, a few hours of studying (if you get to it), a couple of hours at the library for your work study job . . . yeah, it's pretty much the ideal schedule. You've settled into the grind, though, and remember, teachers enjoy a great schedule too.

You begin to realize some things about yourself as a teacher—that one strategy that had worked so well with those second graders completely flopped with the third graders in your class. The Spanish lesson on the perfect past, yep—might have helped if the student understood the present tense! You've gained five pounds although you can't understand why—you barely have time to inhale the lunch you bring, because by the time you walk your students to the lunchroom, get them settled, and then head back, you're already hearing the lunch recess bell ring—oh nuts, you signed up for recess duty that day.

Guess what—teaching isn't easy. You know this. But that's not all—it gets better—you get better. You'll soon be in charge of a classroom and at the helm of and responsible for the learning of all your students.

This book is about getting hired. But getting hired is a big deal—it takes some time, preparation, and serious effort. Getting hired means getting ready to have serious conversations about who you are. Without that knowledge you'll not be able to have a serious conversation with a search committee. People need to know who you are in order to make an informed decision about hiring you.

It's time to turn our attention to getting there. Before you get hired you have to get there—to the district, to the desk of the principal, to the top of the stack of résumés. Getting there takes a whole lot of work. You're going to have to hit the pavement to get your name out there and meet recruiters. There are great teachers out there everywhere. This means you'll need to put in the extra effort to make yourself stand out above the rest.

Getting there means knowing the quintessential tools of the teacher job search: a résumé, cover letter, letters of recommendation, portfolio, license, and transcript. You'll need to know how to talk about your student teaching experiences in ways that are meaningful and reflective. You'll need to demonstrate that you know how to teach, which means a lot more than just content knowledge—it means you know how to inspire students to learn, how to help them up when they stumble, and how to make sure you're reaching everyone in your classroom. Come on, let's get there.

PART 6

Finding Jobs

Projections of Education Statistics to 2019
According to the National Center for Educational Statistics, public school
enrollments will grow by an expected 6 percent between 2007 and 2019. This
national average assumes that some states will have a decrease of 5 percent or more
in enrollments, while some states will have increases greater than 15 percent. Some
geographical areas will experience job growth and add jobs, while some states will
be forced to reduce teaching staff based on numbers. Do you know the trends for
your geographical area?

(http://nces.ed.gov/pubs2011/2011017.pdf)

My To-Do List
1. Get organized for a successful job search and start networking.
2. Find jobs and learn how to read position announcements.
3. Establish a short list of dream jobs and dream working locations.

My Project Overview
1. Take 5: My Dream Teaching Job
2. My ePlanner
   a. *Top 10 Places to Work:* Prioritize and energize your job search.
   b. *My Weekly Summary:* Time once again for your favorite activity.
3. Take 5 Again: Descriptive Statement
4. Take 5 Again: All About Me: Networking Version

It usually happens something like this: Student teaching is in full swing. You didn't realize people could physically work this many hours in a day. You're feeling tired, frustrated that you have to upload another reflection about classroom management, and you're trying to work ahead so you can go to the game this weekend. A pile of papers to be graded is staring you in the face, like the ocular character from the "You could be saving a lot of money with Geico" commercials. You haven't done laundry in over a week and you're down to your last clean button-down shirt (because you've taken our advice from the first part of this book and are dressing like a professional every day). Then BAM! It hits you. Your heart stops. For a moment you feel nothing but sheer joy and excitement. You've just learned that your dream job has been posted with an application deadline of Friday at

5 P.M. Then the reality sets in. Your weekly plans flash before you . . . what can you reschedule? How can you avoid the grading to get your application in on time? You don't even have a résumé written, not to mention a cover letter. You consider calling in sick but you know that would be unethical and you'd just have to make it up at the end of student teaching. What do you do? Apply, of course; you don't need this book to tell you that. But for a moment, let's just pretend you wake up and realize you were dreaming. Fortunately for you, you have this book to help keep you on track and on target for the job search. It's not uncommon though, for a job opening, especially the job you want, to be posted at the most unexpected and inconvenient moment; indeed, most are.

TAKE 5

My Dream Teaching Job

It's not uncommon for employers to ask job candidates what their ideal work environment might look like. Employers are wanting to hear key characteristics of employees—those who are attentive to their needs with respect to content delivery, methods of instruction, and most importantly student learning. You don't have to be modest when you hear this question, and here's why—it can also show your vision for the ideal learning environment, which, after all, is what we want from all teachers. Here's one more thing: this is a good question to energize your job search. You've put a lot of work into your degree; why not "reach for the stars" as it were and start envisioning your dream job? Without a vision, it won't become a reality.

Take 5 minutes to brainstorm key attributes of your dream teaching job. Be as comprehensive as possible and take into account environment, resources, community, colleagues, curriculum, student demographics, achievement data, salary and benefits, housing, opportunities for professional growth.

BEING IN THE RIGHT PLACE AT THE RIGHT TIME

This little adage couldn't be truer for finding your first teaching job. Schools tend to do most of their hiring throughout the spring and the summer. This timing couldn't be more perfect or more problematic for you as a student teacher. If you finish your degree program in December you have plenty of time to ease into the job search, which gets underway in early spring. You might even be fortunate enough to find a district with a mid-year opening or long-term subbing opportunity. If you're student teaching in the spring, you have the added advantage of being an insider in a school while the hiring season is in full swing, giving you ample opportunities to convince the principal that you're the one for the job. Of course all of this means that you'll be actively job-seeking while also making the most of student teaching—you'll be working overtime. When to look for a job isn't the only question new teachers have with respect to timing. You're probably also wondering about how long the process takes and what happens along the way.

THE HIRING CYCLE

Most schools list job vacancies for the following academic year beginning in late winter and early spring. Some districts are better able than others to anticipate vacancies based on variables like district size, the opening of new buildings, and projected retirements. Larger districts tend to do more hiring overall and thus list general vacancies earlier, though they may not know exactly how many vacancies they will have at a particular grade level. Smaller districts tend to err on the side of caution and will wait for more accurate enrollment and staffing projections before listing positions. Don't fret if a smaller to midsize district hasn't listed any positions early in the season—chances are they'll post positions once they have firm numbers.

In addition to figures like enrollment numbers and budgets, school districts often offer positions internally before posting the jobs for new candidates. As a student teacher, you may be privy to some of these conversations, and if you're interested in working for the district where you're student teaching, make it no secret that you're job-seeking. The bottom line is some districts hire year-round but typically by the time fall rolls around and the leaves begin to drop—so too does the number of teaching vacancies posted. That's why the timing of your job search is so important.

66School districts use online application systems. When staffing needs are known, any district administrator can access the online system and review applicant materials. Obviously, it is to your advantage to be on that list. Don't wait until you are finished student teaching—get organized and apply while you are student teaching.**99**

—Jeff McCanna, Human Resources Director

Some districts hire very aggressively, and operate under the assumption that the best candidates in the hard-to-fill areas will be off the market quickly. Plan to be on the market early if you are seeking employment in a competitive school district. For some of you, this may be in the first few weeks of student teaching. Get a head start on your search by being ready with job-seeking materials and regularly searching job vacancies.

Have these key materials ready:

- Résumé
- Cover letter
- Application information (important dates, references, educational information, employer and volunteer contacts)
- Current transcript
- Testing scores or upcoming testing dates
- Standards-based artifacts
- Names of references

These materials are standard parts of the teacher application process. In addition to these materials, most districts require candidates to complete either an online or paper-based standard application. Pay close attention to the directions on employment sites. Not following directions, or leaving a critical piece of requested information out of the process, almost always removes you from consideration.

TIP

Take the application forms very seriously. The manner in which you complete materials tells prospective employers about your professionalism. Employers suggest that you (1) read each question on the application carefully; (2) respond to each question honestly; and (3) proof answers before hitting submit.

PLAN YOUR MOVE

If you're a job candidate who hopes to relocate to a new area, timing is especially important. Advance planning is critical, especially since you may have many additional decisions to make about where to live, moving expenses, and timeline for moving, not to mention how to interview at a distance. Consider your student teaching schedule early; if you plan to make a scouting trip over winter or spring break, advance planning will help you maximize your outcomes on those visits.

TIP

Planning Ahead

Step 1: Make time to find resources

Step 2: Make contact

Step 3: Make travel plans and meet face-to-face

TEACHER LICENSURE AND TEACHER TESTING

Without a doubt, you'll have to occupy yourself with two frequently frustrating and time-consuming aspects of the teacher job search process: licensure and testing.

Because of the decentralized way we do education in this country, each state has its own licensure and certification process to allow individuals to teach in that state. Several states have reciprocal agreements with one another, meaning that teachers trained and licensed in one state are eligible for licensure in another state. It's generally necessary for you to apply for licensure in the state where you're completing your preparation as a teacher and then, following receipt of that license, to pursue certification in another state. Some states require additional coursework upon licensure. Depending on the state, you may have a probationary period to complete that coursework while working as a teacher. Other states are less lenient, and require completion of the coursework prior to applying for licensure. You should be fully aware of the licensure requirements for your area in your state of residency or the state to which you plan to move. Licensure can cause employment headaches, so inform yourself well in advance, and apply early.

Teacher testing is another area of the employment process that can quickly derail a job search. If you plan to seek employment in another state, be sure to inquire about necessary test scores you may need to submit during the application process, or in the first months of employment. Be completely aware of what your prospective employer will expect and need to verify upon your employment. Again, depending on the district and state, you may be able to complete the testing requirements within a given window of time. Others might require all requirements to be met before offering employment. Know what to expect so that if this topic comes up during the application or interview process you're able to provide an answer that demonstrates attention to detail and wherewithal.

JOB SEARCH TIMELINE—THE EARLY BIRD GETS THE WORM

Most job-seeking candidates report a sustained investment of time over the course of student teaching until they were able to find, interview for, and get a job. So don't be discouraged if, especially at the beginning of the job search, things seem to be slow going. Once you do locate a job, by all means apply as soon as possible, but be prepared to hurry up and wait. Some jobs will be listed with a closing date. Closing dates don't mean that interviews start the very next day—sometimes a month will pass before candidates are called to interview. Use closing dates as a general guide. Two weeks is generally a fair amount of time for the job seeker to wait before making a phone call or sending an email about the status of a job application.

Follow-up Attempts

Don't be shy about contacting school districts to check on your application materials. Why? We've all had materials get lost in the mail or disappear into cyber space. It's reassuring to know that they've arrived. While school districts are very busy places, staff are typically very willing respond to a request—if the request is made politely. Before calling, know what you want to ask and then, of course, thank the person for the time and courtesy in providing you the information you needed.

DEVELOP YOUR JOB-SEEKING STRATEGY

Job-seeking is a little like teaching—it's usually not very successful without some planning and forethought. You've already taken a minute to think about what your "dream" or ideal teaching job would be like. Maybe your student teaching placement is ideal—maybe you can't wait to return to your hometown. Whatever the case may be, you must develop a coherent job search strategy and rationale for job-seeking choices and priorities. You're going to be asked lots of questions about who you are as a teacher and what you want. Where do you want to go after this semester? Take a minute to jot down the top 10 districts for which you'd like to teach . . . do it right here in the text, so you're not wasting any time.

_____

_____

_____

_____

_____

Once you establish your top 10, searching for jobs is easy. Don't limit yourself to 10 schools or districts, though. If you're bound to a geographic area, consider all your options, including expanding your commute. The more options you give yourself during the search, the better off you'll be.

Now take a look at that list again. Locate your top districts on a map. Locate all the districts in the immediate vicinity of your top pick. You'd be surprised at how many neighboring districts might also offer similar teaching opportunities. Districts have to be competitive with one another in order to capture the best candidates. If a job in your top district isn't available, consider a neighboring district.

In doing so, several new districts—and potential places of employment—will be located. Keep your options open and do your homework about the opportunities available to you in a given area.

WHERE, OH WHERE, OH WHERE'S THAT JOB?

Teaching jobs are advertised everywhere—in both obvious and less obvious places. We're going to take you to the top six places to start finding jobs so you can begin the process of applying. We encourage you to employ a mixed methods approach to the job search—one that involves multiple strategies and multiple sources of information. Be expansive and exhaustive in your search—you've put a lot of time into your education—now it's time to leave no stone unturned as you seek to find your dream teaching job (and pay off those student loans).

SCHOOL WEBSITES

Remember that short list of your top 10 school districts that you just filled out? If you haven't been checking their websites already, add them to your bookmarks, or favorites tab; you should do that now. Get in the habit of checking these sites frequently. Scour the site for any information—most schools update their job postings as the jobs are made available. Some update every Friday morning at 9:22 A.M.; whenever the site is updated, you should be the first to know—treat it like Wilford Brimley treats his blood sugar—check it, check it often. More recently, some districts have been RSS enabling their employment pages on the website. RSS or Really Simple Syndication is a web feed tool that allows users to "subscribe" to a page or website that is updated frequently. Many blogs employ this tool, so that readers of a particular blog are updated when a new blog post appears. This avoids having to visit each blog each day to check and see if an update has been made to a post or a comment. Some school districts have discovered the usefulness of this tool and now use it to update candidates of new job postings. If a school district utilizes a live feed, or if when you're visiting an employment webpage you notice something that says, "Know when it's new" or "Subscribe to this page," that's a sign that they're using an RSS feed to keep users up-to-date. You'll need to join a service but joining is pretty easy, and most major email companies have simple-to-use "Readers" to help you organize the pages that you've subscribed to. It's a great way to stay ahead of the pack and use your time wisely. Let's make a quick and easy checklist of job resources.

CHECKLIST OF JOB RESOURCES

INTERNET
- Add key sites to your favorites list and check websites often. Establish an RSS reader.

NEWSPAPERS
- Check the classified ads.

WORD-OF-MOUTH
- Tell teachers and other school staff about your search.

SUPERVISOR
- Let your college supervisor know about your dream job—they have contacts, too.

ADMINISTRATORS
- Share your job search plans with the school administrators—they are well-connected and can help you network.

NETWORK
- Tell people who have played key roles in your past. One small lead is all you need.

Districts vary in the amount of detail they share when posting job vacancies. The job announcement below provides significant details about the opening and identifies many of the professional qualities the district seeks in the applicant. It gives you plenty of details to weave into your letter. Take a look.

Position: High School Biology Teacher

Application deadline: March 24, 201x

Submit materials: online @ www.abc.edu

Note: successful candidate must submit fingerprints

Details:
- Teach high school biology courses Grades 9–12.
- Provide high quality biology lesson development that includes lab oriented activities.
- Use a variety of instructional strategies to provide equity and excellence to students of all ability levels.
- Participate in on-going planning, development, and evaluation of curriculum.
- Work cooperatively with other teachers in developing and sharing curriculum strategies, program planning, lab preparation, and team teaching.
- Maintain accurate records and complete all student progress reports and report cards.
- Participate in all staff and department meetings.

Professional Qualifications:

Possess or qualify for immediate issuance of a valid state teaching certificate with an endorsement in biology. Preference will be given to candidates who hold multiple endorsements. Must meet NCLB standard for Highly Qualified teachers.

- Biology degree, B.S. or M.S.
- Experience teaching high school biology courses.
- Experience in student-centered, hands-on learning, and performance-based assessment.
- Experience in using computers/specialized science software.
- Training and/or experience using the cooperative learning "Process Approach" and "Conceptual Approach" in science instruction.
- Interest in team teaching and developing a curriculum with a variety of instruction modes.
- Training, experience, and interest in interdisciplinary teaching.
- Willingness to work with students and staff outside of the regular school day in science related activities.
- Commitment and ability to work with a full range of students including gifted, mainstreamed special education, English language learners, and students from diverse cultural and social backgrounds.
- Ability to meet and maintain punctuality and attendance.
- Experience working with other staff members to accomplish common goals and to develop appropriate instructional strategies.
- Skill in using a variety of instructional strategies to engage student learning through innovative and relevant learning experiences.
- Ability to work in partnership with parents, staff, students, and the community to provide student-centered learning.
- Knowledge of and ability to implement state teaching standards.

Salary and Benefits:

Placement on salary schedule depends on degrees and experience. Comprehensive benefits package—health, vision, dental and life insurance.

Closing Date:

Applications accepted until March 24 or until position is filled.

It's not unusual for schools to post on their website that a fourth grade opening or a high school math position is available. Regardless of how a job posting is written, *include significant details* about your academic training, teaching and related experiences, specialized skills and talents, and your ability to help each child succeed. Always promote yourself. Read between the lines. If a job announcement is terse or doesn't share a great deal about the attributes they're looking for in a candidate, do your homework and try to figure out what they're looking for.

JOB POSTINGS: READ IT! AND WRITE ABOUT IT!

A comprehensive job posting can help you write a convincing cover letter as well as help you prepare fully for an interview. The school is communicating what they expect to see in applicants. For example, here are a few key words and phrases from the job posting:

- Lab-oriented activities; technology skills
- Instructional modes and approaches
- Interdisciplinary teaching and cooperative strategies
- Curriculum awareness
- Hands-on learning
- Differentiated teaching strategies
- Innovative methods
- Student-centered philosophy and specific content beliefs
- Awareness of standards
- Contribute to activities before/after school
- Performance-based instruction
- Community interaction
- Strong content base
- Committed to being there and being on time

TIP

Job announcements can provide the lead you want. Read the ad carefully and follow the directions. If the ad is comprehensive, there will be a number of key words and phrases that you'll want to use in your application materials.

COOPERATING TEACHERS

Schools are close networks of individuals, and you'd be hard pressed to find a tighter knit group of teammates. Teachers look out for their own—and if they think you have what it takes, they'll do everything in their power to help get you a job. So don't keep it a secret that you're looking. Not to mention that teachers are well-springs of information about other schools in a community or urban area. Teachers also network, so even if they can't find a job for you in their school or community, they may know a teacher down the road who may be able to help you out. Utilize your cooperating teachers—they're a great resource.

TIP

Start talking about your job search to your cooperating teacher and others in the school district.

It's like having the "cellular network" helping you out.

Word of mouth is a powerful job seeking strategy.

STUDENT TEACHING SUPERVISOR

Aside from giving you hives as they supervise your on-site teaching, your supervisor should be able to give you good insight into the teaching market, at least in that geographic area. In our experience, supervisors have been a great resource for student teachers, particularly those teachers working in communities and at locations outside of the general scope of their teacher preparation program. International teaching supervisors, and those working at special sites, often have insider information and most importantly good contact information because they are often in touch with multiple hiring officials throughout the schools in which they supervise student teachers. Be honest with your supervisor about where you want to work, and don't be afraid to ask questions.

BUILDING ADMINISTRATORS

Just the thought of asking anything of the building administrator(s) where you're student teaching probably makes you feel uncomfortable, let alone asking them for a job—no way! Right? Wrong! You're gonna have to get over this one, because building administrators are a great resource for you when it comes to finding jobs. First off—many of you would love to just stay put and keep teaching where you're student teaching. Not every building will have openings, though. If you've made a good impression, you'd be surprised at how many administrators are willing to hit the pavement for you and share your contact information with their close colleagues making hiring decisions. Many candidates report getting an interview and eventually a job offer as a result of a contact they made through their student teaching administrator.

COMMUNITY NETWORKING

Family friends, relatives, neighbors, local business people, past employers, high school classmates, former K–12 teachers—all of these people are potential resources. With all the tools that are available over the Internet, there's no excuse for not making connections with these individuals. A quick phone call to let them know you are seeking a job may be the best approach for some. If you have their email send a brief email message with your résumé attached. This communication may lead to a job opening or it may lead to just a friendly hello. If you approach people in the right way, you'll be surprised how helpful they can be. Most of us like to help when we can. The few minutes it takes to network could be career changing.

ARE YOU NET (OR NOT) WORKING?

Take this simple yes/no quiz to see if you are indeed net (or not) working and engaging your potential employment networks.

1. I engage in discussions about my job seeking interests with my student teaching team (includes cooperating teacher, supervisor, peers, administrators, and professors).
   ☐ yes   ☐ no

2. I have sent a formally written letter or email expressing my job-seeking goals to all potential leads.
   ☐ yes   ☐ no

3. I have established a "short list" and "long list" of potential employer contacts.
   ☐ yes   ☐ no

4. I am aware of opportunities to meet recruiters at job fairs and other events, and plan to attend.
   ☐ yes   ☐ no

5. I am seeking opportunities within my student teaching placement to meet teachers, administrators, and school personnel at workshops, professional development seminars, and building/district meetings.
   ☐ yes   ☐ no

6. I have prepared a short "All About Me—Networking Version" to whip out when introduced to others who may be potential allies in my job-seeking process (see the following section).
   ☐ yes   ☐ no

TAKE 5 **AGAIN**

All About Me: Networking Version

The number one most popular first interview question is the one that begins something like, "Tell me a little about yourself." That question can be a deal maker or breaker. You should prepare a networking version of that question, so when you're introduced to people you're not stumbling over words to tell them who you are, and why you're there . . . oh, yeah, and that you're looking for a job.

When you introduce yourself or are introduced here are the three things you want to be sure someone hears:

> • Your name   • Your school   • Completion date

> *Hi, I'm Juan Hernandez from Anywhere College, and I'm student teaching with Estelle for the next 10 weeks. After that I'll be looking for a teaching job in the area. Do you have any suggestions where I might start?*

See, that wasn't so hard. How about this one:

> *Hello. I'm Ruth Walker and I'm a student teacher from the University of Anytown this semester in Lucy Brown's classroom.*

Of course, both of these examples assume you'll be introducing yourself. Chances are your cooperating teacher will take the lead on introducing you. Remember to smile, shake hands, and make a good first impression.

All about me—notes to self: smile, shake hands, and smile some more.

Remember to mention my name, my school, and degree completion date.

Hi,

Or,
Hello, It's a pleasure to meet you. I'm

Did I sound awake? Excited about meeting this person? Engaged? Let's hope so!

SUMMARY

Finding Jobs

Student teaching ends up being an incredibly busy experience for most student teachers. Part 6: Finding Jobs is all about pooling your resources and exhausting every option as you prioritize and get organized for a successful job search. As we mentioned in the text—the early bird really does get the worm. Those who make the biggest investment in a successful job search are almost always guaranteed the biggest rewards. The following activities are designed to help you make the most of your search.

ON THE WEB

ePlanner Activities

1. *Top 10 Places to Work:* Prioritize and energize your job search.
2. *My Weekly Summary:* Time once again for your favorite activity.

eResources

Visit: *www.edweek/org/tm* to review opportunities in education and locate districts ready to hire.

Visit the interactive state Department of Education map resource to find out about licensure and testing requirements in each state.

eJournal

1. Have a conversation with your cooperating teacher, university supervisor, or other mentor from your teacher preparation program about the resources they used to find jobs. Write a bit about what they tell you, and pay close attention to any networking tips they might share with you.
2. We're living in a digital age with all kinds of neat and exciting tools at our disposal to meet and connect with new people. What are the benefits for you as a job seeker when using these technologies? What are the dangers?
3. What social media do you use to create a professional web presence?

PART 7

Résumés That Hit the Target

Dr. Mario Andrade, Assistant Superintendent says: "I want to see a well-organized résumé so that I can get information in a glance. I have to look at it very quickly, so what's the essence? What can that person teach and do they have diverse experiences?"

My To-Do List

1. Incorporate the characteristics of successful teachers into your résumé.
2. Prioritize your key material and make every line count.
3. Create a convincing profile on one page.

My Project Overview

1. Take 5: The 30-Second Test
2. My ePlanner
   a. *Résumé Samples and Templates*
   b. *My Weekly Summary:* Because writing a résumé isn't enough.
3. Take 5 Again: Your Résumé Draft

Your résumé is usually a recruiter's first glimpse into who you are as a potential candidate. You have just one page to tell them where you've been, what you've done, and most importantly, what you will do. This chapter will aim to get you on track by focusing on the three most important characteristics or target points of a résumé—your objective and special skills (what you want to teach and why you can teach it); your education and academic background (degrees earned); and experiences (employment, volunteer, and related experiences that make you qualified or able to begin the position).

TAKE 5

The 30-Second Test

Most employers will spend about 30 seconds with each résumé the first time around. Keep in mind that the employer probably won't read every word. That's right, 30 seconds. That's a discouraging thought given the time you spend in writing your résumé, but it's no exaggeration. So—since you have only 30 seconds to catch the employer's attention—make your résumé worth reading. Given that you only have 30 seconds to convince an employer that you're the next John Dewey, take 5 minutes to think about three things an employer absolutely must know about you. If you don't know who John Dewey is, take another 5 to find out. You should know him!

❝Make sure your résumé is the most up to date piece of information you provide with all of your strong selling points. It's your calling card—put your best foot forward. Make sure it sells you in an accurate way, with plenty of information which we can use.❞

—Dr. Jake Chung, Principal

If your résumé doesn't measure up, sending it to hiring officials is a bit like shooting blanks. Don't let your résumé be a shot in the dark.

Teaching Objective
Education
Experience
What have you done?
What can you do?
College experience
specialized training
What you want to teach?
Why can you teach it?

THE FIRST 10 PERCENT: RÉSUMÉ CONTACT INFORMATION

The easiest part of writing your résumé can also be the most important part—your contact information. Believe it or not, we hear from recruiters every year who tell us that they were prepared to call a candidate in for an interview only to find that the cell phone number they gave was no longer working (or the message on the other end was inappropriate). In addition to your name, your address, telephone, and email are all important contacts to provide. Some candidates go overboard and oversize their name. We encourage you to use the same size font as the rest of the résumé. Double check your address, and be sure to provide the correct mailing address. If you plan to move but aren't yet sure of your future address, use the most current residing address. Some students use their parent's mailing address during a period of transition. The great thing is that you can then contact the district again to update them on your new mailing address. Having excuses to make contacts is a good thing. Also, make sure your email address is appropriate. It should easily identify you and should be some professional derivation of your name. If your full name is unavailable, use initials. For security reasons, never use your birthdate or year in an email address. Also avoid email addresses that are intended to be funny, sexy, or related to alcohol or drugs. Lastly, if you have an ePortfolio address related to your teacher preparation program, this is a great place to list it. Good news—you've already written 10 percent of your résumé. What follows next depends on your preparation and background.

THE NEXT 30 PERCENT: TEACHING OBJECTIVE

The best teaching objectives are those that immediately inform the reader about what you want to teach. Avoid statements about what you wish to obtain, what your teaching preferences are, and your lofty career goals. Don't make a recruiter or hiring official wonder what it is you can do. Just cut to the chase. The following objective statements do just that.

Bilingual Preschool	Elementary Education, Grades K–6
Behavior Disorder Specialist, K–12	Business Education and Technology
Middle School Reading Teacher	English Teacher and Debate Coach
Social Studies: World History, Economics: Model UN Sponsor	Journalism and Film Teacher: Yearbook Sponsor
Spanish Teacher, 7–12; Soccer Coach	Home Economics/Health Teacher
Music: Instrumental and Vocal	Mathematics: AP and Honors Calculus

TIP

An executive director of human resources told a roomful of student teachers, "Résumés with strong beginnings tend to get read thoroughly. Tell me what you can teach. No philosophical statements; no career aspirations; no long-term goals. I'll get to that in the interview."

State What You Can Teach, Coach, and Sponsor

The more you have to offer a district the more marketable you'll be—it's a simple fact. With shrinking budgets and a need for teachers who are both flexible and multi-talented, many candidates find additional endorsements and a willingness to coach or sponsor school related activities help to pave the way for interviews and potential offers. Your teaching objective should also indicate a willingness to do these extracurricular sorts of things; you'd be surprised at the number of candidates who get offers because of that extra after-school vacancy they're able to fill. If you go one step farther and list your teaching skills or competencies, you will set yourself apart from all other candidates. Take a look at Bea Goode's résumé and notice that it quickly tells an employer about her teaching objective, skills, and after-school interests.

BEA GOODE
....

OBJECTIVE & SKILLS: ELEMENTARY EDUCATION, GRADES K–6

- Multifaceted literacy development approach in reading, writing, listening, speaking, technology
- Family involvement by connecting kids to their communities, and communities to their kids
- Global readiness incorporated into classroom learning—speak three languages
- Diverse learners and diverse approaches: individualized instruction and multiple adaptations

SPONSOR: Intramurals, soccer and school-related functions

Most hiring officials wear many hats in their school district. Anything that can make their job easier improves your chances to get noticed. Candidates who take the time to clearly identify a teaching objective as well as special interests, skills or competencies improve their chances of getting an interview. *Keep your eye on the target and don't miss the mark on this one.* A teaching objective is a simple statement about *what you want to teach*—not your philosophy or motivations for teaching—we'll get to that later.

A Secret Target

If you take the time to determine specific skills and competencies that you can bring to a teaching setting, you have already positioned yourself to answer several key interview questions. And you are only in the résumé writing stage.

Let's take one more look at Bea Goode. Imagine Bea sitting down with a principal for an interview. At some point during their conversation, it's a sure thing that the principal will ask Bea questions like these: *"Why should I hire you?"* or *"What can you bring to our school that other applicants don't have?"* or *"Name three strengths that you possess."* Do you get it? Do you see why this section of your résumé is so critical? It can set you up for success long before you receive the phone call to schedule an interview time.

BEA GOODE

OBJECTIVE & SKILLS: ELEMENTARY EDUCATION, GRADES K–6

- Multifaceted literacy development approach in reading, writing, listening, speaking, technology
- Family involvement by connecting kids to their communities, and communities to their kids
- Global readiness incorporated into classroom learning—speak three languages
- Diverse learners and diverse approaches: individualized instruction and multiple adaptations

SPONSOR: Intramurals, soccer and school-related functions

Bea has already positioned herself to answer the question "Why should I hire you?" In Bea's voice, she can talk about her abilities to work with diverse learners in a variety of settings using a multifaceted literacy approach that incorporates technology. She could expand her answer by addressing the need to work closely with families and, if possible, conversing in their native tongue.

THE NEXT 30 PERCENT: YOUR EDUCATIONAL BACKGROUND

The educational and academic background section of your résumé should succinctly communicate your academic preparation and potential. Most people are not aware of the "potential" piece in this section. If you stated your degree details including date of graduation, institution, and year, it's a one-liner and another 10 percent of your résumé.

Candidates who state their most recent degree first, with correct annotations (dates, major, minor, specializations, and certificates), followed by valuable academic experiences, including study abroad, membership in honors associations, other academic accolades, and relevant coursework that relates directly to the stated objective, have provided a rich picture of their scholarly abilities and probable teaching competencies.

Let's look at the Education section of Hirem E. Soon's résumé. Most résumés would state the following:

EDUCATION:	MA	Special Education, State University, August 201x
	BA	Social Work & Spanish, Private College, May 201x

Three important facts are apparent about Hirem: he's qualified to teach special education; has a background in social work; and there's a good chance that he is fluent in Spanish. This information is solid and would put Hirem in many administrators' in-box. But, there is an easy way to increase his chances for being noticed—simply tell the hiring official a bit more about Hirem. Let's add the following:

International Study: Alicante, Spain, 201x; Mexico City, Mexico, 201x

International Exchange: Rotary Exchange Student, Lima, Peru, 201x

Honors: *magna cum laude*, President's List, Phi Beta Kappa

Special Education Coursework: Parent-Teacher Communication, Characteristics of Disabilities, Practicum with Exceptional Persons, Behavioral and Social Interventions, Strategist I Methods, Assessment of Learning Differences, Advanced Reading Clinic, Direct Instruction-Academic Skills, Explicit Instruction, Transition & Related Issues

With the addition of these details to Hirem's résumé, the potential employer has learned that Hirem is aware of other cultures, has excelled academically, and has completed a preparation program that has provided a rich background in both pedagogy and practice in his teaching area. It only took Hirem a few minutes to include this information. The results may pay off immediately in the outcome of his job search.

Unless your high school was of a unique nature such that it may have prepared you well for a particular teaching environment (e.g., boarding school or an international school) to which you are applying, do not list high school attendance or information about graduation. One other note: academic background does not include part-time work or random coursework. Employers value employment history, but save work experiences for the application form.

30 PERCENT TO GO: EXPERIENCE

Employers look at a candidate's experience to determine fit. How this experience is presented on a résumé is critical. By describing experiences in some detail and by drawing on specific teaching materials or teaching strategies, the employer can get a glimpse of you in the classroom. Employers want to know how you will help each student be successful in academic endeavors, social situations, and behavior management. Giving the employer a dynamic description of your approaches, technologies, methods, theories, and processes can convince an employer that you are believable, capable, and indeed, qualified to step into this important classroom.

> **TIP**
>
> Jeff McCanna, Human Resources Director, who reviews thousands of résumés every year, reminds job seekers that "giving an employer a good picture of your unique experiences in the classroom makes you more believable and certainly more interesting as a candidate."

Employers know that all students in field experiences and internship settings create and teach a lesson plan. By providing a detailed description of your lesson plan that includes strategies, outcomes, materials, adaptations, and assessments, you demonstrate knowledge that teaching is multifaceted and thus you've taken your résumé to the next level of quality. You might even be close to hitting the mark.

Descriptive Statements

Hirem has given the employer a clear view into his teaching style, knowledge, and classroom environment by using rich descriptors to describe his internship.

Behavior Disorders Internship, West High School, Fall 201x

- Facilitated individualized goal-setting in learning and self-monitoring for students in BD class
- Utilized effective behavior management and de-escalation strategies
- Collaborated with speech pathologists, agency support specialists, homeroom teachers, and others to promote successful outcomes and achievement of goals in students' educational plans
- Integrated multiple assistive technology software programs to assist student learning
- Procured municipal grant to cover expenses for two-day education excursion to Chicago for students who met eight week behavior and learning goals

> **TIP**
>
> **Make your résumé work for you.** It's all in the details—lesson plan details. Include:
>
> - Strategies
> - Outcomes
> - Materials
> - Adaptations
> - Assessments

Hirem used specific descriptors to highlight best practices in his experience. Rich descriptors that draw on your unique experiences in the classroom are

- more believable,
- more effective, *and certainly*
- more interesting for the employer.

In the above example, each descriptor begins with an action verb—facilitated, utilized, collaborated, integrated, procured, etc. Active verbs keep the interest of the reader and provides energy to your document.

TIP

Don't be passive.

Express your knowledge, accomplishments, and achievements in dynamic, meaningful words.

TAKE 5 **AGAIN**

Descriptive Statement

Keep an employer interested in your résumé by giving them something worth reading. Take 5 minutes and write four or five descriptive statements that reflect your teaching responsibilities. Remember that ePlanner activity about your content area, My Content Area? Be sure to reference that page now as you describe your teaching. You need to look like someone in your field.

Volunteer and Service Experiences in Your Résumé

Employers are looking for individuals who have a variety of experiences both in the classroom and outside the classroom. Employers know that individuals who have volunteered in community-building activities with a diverse segment of people will be better able to reach out to students, parents, families and staff. Let the employer know that you have worked with individuals and organizations in both the community and campus setting.

TIP

Employers want to see experience in the classroom and community. Employers want to read about someone who has engaged with children and families in diverse settings. Why do employers want to see this on a résumé? Exposure to dissimilar people introduces cultural diversity and allows for different ways of thinking about experiences.

Résumés Use Action Phrases

Résumé-writing breaks a conventional writing rule: no complete sentences. By using complete sentences, the résumé will be loaded with phrases like these: I created . . . I produced . . . I motivated . . . I did . . . Beginning sentences with "I" puts the focus on you and not on the importance of your activity or accomplishment. Read the phrases below and you'll see how the material becomes repetitive and passive when it starts with a personal pronoun. In the no-no example below, notice that you have to read three words to get to the really juicy stuff . . . Remember the 30-second rule. Think back to your 7th grade Language Arts class . . . you know the one where you memorized all those helping verbs (am, is, are, have, has, had, and so on)—well, your résumé is one place where those kinds of verbs aren't much help. You should strive to use words that end in "ed"!

NO NO!

- I have guided an outdoor art education workshop . . .
- I have prepared lessons to reflect everyday activities . . .
- I was selected to serve as a representative on . . .
- I was active in the community volunteer program . . .

The following examples demonstrate how to use action words to describe significant responsibilities. Notice that when you quickly read the descriptive phrases, you can feel the *action* in the teaching activity.

YES YES!

- Communicated regularly with parents through classroom blog, student-produced podcasts, web-conferencing project, and student ePortfolios
- Focused and redirected students in need of behavior and learning support to promote better outcomes in learning and positive behaviors exhibited during eight week secondary placement
- Guided the design of a student-led community service project at the Free Lunch Project to encourage positive self-image through helping others

Action words give your résumé life and vigor. The best résumés, of course, use a variety of action words to describe teaching experiences. It's not uncommon to have very specific targeted lingo in a teaching area. Use words that are industry-specific; your "industry-specific" words are all education-based. There are hundreds, even thousands of action words to consider.

Category Headings Help You Hit the Target, Too

Category headings introduce your material to a reader. And, without question, help you to individualize your résumé. Category headings also help you to keep all of your information organized in distinct areas on your document and will help focus the employer's attention on your qualifications. There can be any number of category headings but the ones most commonly used include *Objective, Education, Competencies, Teaching Experience, Activities, Service, Employment,* and *References.*

Objective + Education + Experience = Your Professional Image

The résumé helps to shape an employer's image of you. Think of it as a powerful marketing tool that promotes your abilities, one which succinctly tells employers who you are, what you have done, and how you can fulfill their needs. If you have concentrated on the three key components of teaching objective, education and experience, you'll hit your mark . . . sure thing. Why, because other people will take shortcuts and produce résumés that look like a car salesman's. Take a look at the warning below.

Warning! Don't be tempted to copy a résumé template from the web or from a software program. Templates are general in nature—yup, you guessed it—your résumé will look general in nature if you use one. And, it will look like most other applicants' résumés for a business job—not a teaching job.

So, let's make this simple. Here are 10 sure-fire pointers to help you hit the target.

10 QUICK RÉSUMÉ WRITING POINTERS

1. Select a common font. Size 10 is optimal.
2. Use ample margins and sufficient spacing; white spaces enhance the overall appearance; but too much white can send the wrong message.
3. Describe your experiences with action phrases; use words like *Created, Organized, Supervised,* and *Developed.*
4. Avoid using the same verbs or actions word (developed . . . developed . . . developed).
5. Use concrete words rather than vague descriptions to illustrate experiences.
6. Pay attention to your grammar, punctuation, and spelling. The final copy must be error-free.
7. Be consistent in how you format your entries (use the same approach for dates: either 08/201x or Fall 201x). Double check for consistency in punctuation.
8. Most résumés are one page in length. If two pages are necessary, the second page should include your name and the page number.
9. List references including their contact information on a separate page. The page should begin with your name and the words "Reference Listing."
10. Save your résumé as a .doc or .docx as well as a .pdf. Use the .pdf for online applications. To send a copy of your resume to an employer or to take to an interview, print your résumé on white 8½ × 11 paper. Save and regularly update your résumé.

Don't Forget to Take Your Résumé to the Interview

Job seekers who realize the value of a well-designed résumé are already ahead of their competitors. If you clearly show a reader what you can do and what you know, chances are you'll be better able to talk about your knowledge and skills at an interview. It's already on paper—you've already articulated this information—so in effect, you have a cheat sheet right in front of you.

Remember to take several copies with you to the interview. You may meet with a number of individuals who have not had the opportunity to review your résumé. Share it with others just as you would a business card.

TIP

Nerves . . . nerves . . . nerves . . .

Having your résumé with you allows you to review your strengths and your details about student teaching before your interview.

And, it doesn't look like a cheat sheet.

TAKE 5 **AGAIN**

Résumé Draft

The hardest part of writing a résumé is making sure you get all the important details out. We have samples and templates available on-line that are proven winners on the market. Take 5 minutes to get a jump-start on your résumé by brainstorming key information below. Write in the text and transfer to a template later. It's that easy.

Teaching objective:

Coaching objective: (drama, sports, debate)

Interests and special skills: use space below to identify what makes you stand out.

Education: record key details, include institution, degree, date, major, minor, honors, license

    Institution:

    Degree/date:

    Major/minor:

    Honors:

    Licensure:

    International study:

    Place, dates, area of study:

Relevant coursework: (list key courses that strengthen your teaching objective)

Experiences: (list major teaching and related experiences with action descriptions)

Clinical/field experiences

Student teaching internship

Related experiences:

Youth-related experiences; campus/community service; volunteerism

SUMMARY

Résumés That Hit the Target

For most job-seeking candidates, the résumé is an employer's first glimpse into you as an individual. Application forms don't allow you flexibility and the ability to show off your personality—from a design perspective (how your résumé looks visually), to the way you describe your experiences. In our experience, a well polished and effective résumé is like getting dressed up in a suit—it sets the stage for a productive interview and demonstrates professionalism. Your résumé will become a life-long career chronicle. Make the investment now in a polished résumé—the following activities will help.

ON THE WEB

ePlanner Activities

1. *Résumé Sample and Template:* Elementary School.
2. *Résumé Sample and Template:* Middle School.
3. *Résumé Sample and Template:* High School.
4. *My Weekly Summary:* Because writing a résumé isn't enough.

eJournal

1. One or more of your descriptive phrases in your résumé should address differentiated instruction. Write in more detail about how you differentiated materials, provided accommodations, and used resource experts to help you with this. Employers want to see evidence of collaboration to meet individual students' needs. Share an experience from your student teaching.

eResources

1. Résumé action words
2. Résumé category headings

Video Tips

Listen in as an employer gives sound advice on crafting cover letters and résumés that hit the mark.

PART 8

Letters and Employer Communication

Even in this digital age, cover letters play an important role. A good cover letter can grab the interest of a busy human resources director or a harried principal. Tell a story—tell your story! What makes you qualified for this teaching position? In what ways will you help students succeed? How and with whom will you build meaningful relationships? Don't cut corners on this important marketing tool. Put effort into your letter. Powerful letters get noticed. This in turn means that you will get noticed. Get it?

My To-Do List

1. Consider your letter of application and other communications with employers as important marketing tools.
2. Promote your abilities through details unique to your experience and preparation.
3. Understand the difference between informal communication and formal job-seeking etiquette.

My Project Overview

1. Take 5: My Passion Story
2. My ePlanner
   a. *Letter Builder:* Building a letter with three parts.
   b. *Letter Sample and Template.*
   c. *My Weekly Summary:* Find inspiration for your letters in your weekly overview.
3. Take 5 Again: My "For Example" Story

NEWTCHR@coldmail.com: OMG! R U LOOKING 4 A NEW EL-ED TCHR? IM HQ – HIRE ME PLS! I WAN2TLK 2 U ASAP. R U G2B @ TCHR JBFAIR? WLD L2MEET U F2F 2 TLK ABT JOB! TTYL!

Prinskinner@Springfieldschools.edu: WE ARE NOT LOOKING ANYMORE.

If you can read and (at least partially) understand the message above, it's very important that you read this chapter, because chances are, you've grown up in the Internet, text message, MTV generation. That puts you at high risk of ST^ (Screwing things up) when it comes to making important professional contacts. Seems like a no-brainer, right? Well, not so, according to the recruiters we work with. In fact too many applicants exhibit unprofessional—and even immature—behaviors with respect to their communications with recruiters. You've only got one chance to make the best impression possible; don't blow it by momentarily slipping into SMS/Twitter mode with potential employers. Trust us, they won't be LOL!

TAKE 5

My Passion Story

Every employer needs to see your passion before making you an offer. Think back to that reflective exercise at the beginning of the book—the one where we asked you to write about why you decided to become a teacher. Let's revisit that topic again but this time talk about why you made it through your teacher preparation program, what inspires you about teaching and making a difference with kids—what's your motivation, and why do you possess a passion for teaching?

Ninety percent of all written correspondence with potential employers will take the form of a cover letter. You might find yourself uploading a pdf version of your letter, attaching it to an email or sending it the good old fashioned way—through the mail. All of that depends on how your potential employer wishes to receive the letter. Let's examine what goes into a cover letter, how to make a cover letter convincing, and most importantly, how you can land an interview with one.

There are three things to know about letter writing:

1. letters give voice to your résumé,
2. letters tell your story,
3. letters can portray competence.

Let's use these three simple points to talk about job search letters. There is nothing magical here—just some good, solid advice about a very old and revered practice—the art of letter writing—you might ask your grandparents about it.

Letters give voice to your résumé. No, we're not talking about those record-able greeting cards. In fact, avoid those at all cost. So whose voice?—well, yours. You bet. In a cover letter your voice can be heard, even if the letter is just three paragraphs long; it can be convincing, thoughtful, persuading, and motivating. On the other hand, it can be dull and completely laborious to read.

One of the easiest ways to give voice to your letter is to write and speak it at the same time. Does it sound like you? Are there transitions? Can you identify key points, much like a thesis? Is there a sense of rhythm that moves you along? Do you feel the excitement about your passion? About your desire to help students succeed? Are you painting a picture of what your classroom feels like, looks like? Are parents included? Differentiated learning techniques? Technology? Collaborators? Write as if you are telling a story about yourself.

Letters tell a story. Written words are powerful. Words that are carefully chosen will clearly communicate your thoughts, beliefs, and unique experiences. Chances are if you spend just a bit more time on your letter than you had planned, you'll create a piece that talks to the reader. A well-developed story has a beginning or introduction, a middle section (the plot), and of course, the reason you are suited for the job—the ending. A good story line will incorporate your voice, your commitment to the future of education, and your dedication to best practices and student success.

Employers say it!

In the simplest terms, a cover letter

- represents you,
- introduces you,
- can open the door for an interview.

All of the above is true *if* the letter makes a positive impression.

LETTERS ARE OFTEN THE ACHILLES' HEEL IN THE APPLICATION PROCESS

A poor letter . . .

Tells too much or too little and quickly finds its way into the employer's rejection stack or trash bin.

Employers bemoan the fact that many cover letters are pitiable writing. Surely job seekers understand that the cover letter has the same significance as the application form, the résumé, and the interview portfolio (Part 9). Take note: employers are not going to waste their precious time asking for something they don't need or won't examine closely. Be careful of sample Internet letters. Those letters, while perhaps fine in form, often completely miss the point when it comes to communicating those characteristics important in the teacher job search. Employers value letters that show intimate details of one's growth as a new teacher—the things you've learned during student teaching and how you hope to make a huge impact in the lives of the children in the employer's school.

TIP

Don't slip up by taking shortcuts in writing a job seeking letter. Slow down and get it right.

Letters can portray confidence and competence. It's true. The letter—good or bad—will have a persona of its own. The syntax, punctuation, and vocabulary frame the information and illustrate how your experiences have guided your actions and philosophy. Your confidence can be displayed by giving specifics about a lesson plan, an assessment, or students' reaction to an activity. Perhaps your cooperating teacher plans to incorporate your idea into the curriculum for next year. Employers want to hear this kind of detail. Think of it this way—in real estate it's location, location, location. In letter writing, it's detail, detail, detail.

We know that just the thought of writing letters creates anxiety for many job seekers. It might help you to know that employers are not interested in fancy phrases or ingenious approaches. They want the basics: why you are writing, what you have to offer, how you can help their students succeed.

❝*As a job seeker, you are always trying to put your best foot forward, to sell yourself to a potential employer. Why not spend a few more minutes putting a quality letter together? You spend hours on a résumé; please expend that same energy on a letter. It may change the course of your career.*❞

—Dr. Kristin Rickey, Superintendent

GETTING STARTED ON THE LETTER

OK. So you've never written a letter for a serious reason. You are feeling a bit uncomfortable, even inadequate about talking about yourself in a few paragraphs. You might even resort to some of these excuses:

- I don't have time.
- I don't know what to say.
- I'd rather just send a quick email or even drop by the building.
- I have writer's block.

How do I start a letter and what will get the reader's attention? Let's not agonize over an attention-grabbing first sentence. Get it out of the way quickly. There's nothing wrong with just stating the facts:

> *I am writing to express my interest in the elementary teaching position posted on the Central School District website. I will complete my Bachelor of Arts Degree with teaching certification from State University in May, 201x, and am particularly interested in the CSD because of its strong academic and extracurricular programs, commitment to diversity, and talented teaching staff. My field experiences in education as well as my volunteer-related positions have allowed me to gain valuable skills and perspectives on teaching.*

Once the opening line and paragraph are done, you can begin your story. Remember all the essays and book reviews you crafted in English classes that focused on the protagonist and the role of this central figure's character development and the resulting dialogue and its effect on story development. You know where we are going with this. You are the protagonist—it's your life we are talking about. *Can you talk to the reader—the potential employer—through your words?* It's hard to remember a central figure if there are limited details or bland and uneventful story lines.

**Make your letter be more than words,
more than a few isolated paragraphs.
*Make it speak.***

What led you to teaching? How has your philosophy been formed? What specific motivational strategies empowered your students to successfully accomplish the goals of the lesson? What specific resources did you employ to make the lesson come alive and have particular significance to the students? In what ways did you share the outcomes with families? Talking about and writing about these topics can give your letter a voice.

THE BODY OF THE LETTER

The significant part of the letter, typically referred to as the body of the letter, is where you can share your story with employers. The body of the letter allows you to sell yourself as someone competent and passionate about teaching. Think of ways you can do the same as you begin to visualize your letter.

> *I recently completed my student teaching at Creekside Academy, primarily in first grade, and I have also spent time in third and fourth-grade classrooms. Overall, I was involved in setting the foundation of reading, writing, spelling and math skills for first graders. Specifically, I worked with several teaching curricula and methods, including Guided Reading, 6+1 Writing Traits, PWIM, Working with Words, Think Aloud's, and MOSS kits, a hands-on science program. While creating lesson plans, I made sure to address the state teaching standards and the Creekside benchmarks. I created and was involved in the development of various assessment tools to gauge student progress, performed running records, and observed other assessment tests that the school district requires, including Basic Reading Inventory and Observational Survey. In addition, I practiced Positive Behavior Support throughout my teaching experiences for all students and created an original unit called "Wild about Weather," taught with technology whenever possible; additionally, I wrote original poetry, songs and a children's book to enhance my lessons (to view: www.goode.portfolio.net).*
>
> *My cooperating teacher and I attended an educational workshop on how best to meet the needs of students with developmental delays. This reinforced my own teaching philosophy—every child has a unique set of strengths and needs; therefore, a teacher cannot assume that students are all on the same level at any one given time. I have been able to apply this knowledge by working closely with students on IEP's, including a boy with autism in our class, which was a remarkable experience. Overall, throughout all of my teaching experiences, I focused my teaching objectives on the diverse learning styles of children including differentiated learning and balanced literacy.*

The body of your letter is often your one chance to spark an employer's interest in you—to show your passion for teaching and learning. Remember your teaching philosophy? Why you want to be a teacher—make sure a bit of that shines through here. Employers like your stories—they make you real, they make your teaching genuine, they invite the reader into your classroom and indeed your philosophy.

TAKE 5 **AGAIN**

My "For Example" Story

Details are the proof in the pudding when it comes to getting your first teaching job. Without specific examples from your student teaching and field experiences to rely on, employers have no real way of knowing if you're the right candidate. Your letter should be full of details, not boring jargon. Take 5 minutes to write one experience from student teaching that motivated you to rise to the challenge or that was a considerable learning event in your development as a teacher. Why do you want to share this with an employer?

(Note to writer: this can go in your letter)

GETTING TO THE END OF MY LETTER

Just a few sentences left, but important ones. This is your last chance to convince the employer that you are both competent and interested in the job. This is where you reinforce that your skills match the job posting; this is where—with humility—you state why you think you are the best person for the opening.

Maintain enthusiasm and professionalism through to the end of the letter. Don't get sloppy, don't take the easy way out. Express yourself; leave no question in the readers' mind that you can do this job.

I am ready to use my strengths and talents to offer students the best education possible. That being said, I continue to enhance my skills by taking additional reading seminars. My education, coupled with my teaching experiences, has more than prepared me for the openings at Central Elementary, particularly my experience working with multi-age classrooms that align well with Central's Basic School philosophy. I am very interested in meeting with you at your convenience, and I want to thank you for your time and consideration. My résumé and application were submitted online as requested on your website. I look forward to hearing from you.

OK. Almost finished. Set your letter aside, do something else, and come back to proof it before you send it off. Spell checkers are good but not fool-proof, so you need to be the final reader.

PROOF, PROOF, PROOF, PROOF, PROOF

A quick proof . . .
Double check names, places and relevant information on the web.

- Capitalization of names, dates, places
- Spelling and grammar check
- Correct names and professional titles (Dr., Ms., Mr.) and school names
- Accurate details, descriptions, dates
- Margins consistent—top, bottom, sides—typically 1" margins
- Paragraph structure
- Proper closing, using Sincerely or Sincerely yours
- Font is easy to read and common

LET'S LOOK AT THE LETTER IN TOTALITY—START TO FINISH

Your Street Address   *(Return Address)*
Your City, State, Zip
Date

Person, Title   *(Inside Address)*
Institution or School
City, State, Zip

Dear Put Name Here: *(Salutation)*

I am writing to express my interest in the elementary teaching position posted on the Central School District website. I will complete my Bachelor of Arts Degree with teaching certification from State University in May, 201x, and am particularly interested in CSD because of its strong academic and extracurricular programs, commitment to diversity, and talented teaching staff. My field experiences in education as well as my volunteer-related positions have allowed me to gain valuable skills and perspectives on teaching.

I recently completed my student teaching at Creekside Academy, primarily in first grade, and I have also spent time in third- and fourth-grade classrooms. Overall, I was involved in setting the foundation of reading, writing, spelling and math skills for first graders. Specifically, I worked with several teaching curricula and methods, including Guided Reading, 6+1 Writing Traits, PWIM, Working with Words, Think Aloud's, and MOSS kits, a hands-on science program. While creating lesson plans, I made sure to address Common Core standards and the Creekside benchmarks. I created and was involved in the development of various assessment tools to gauge student progress, performed running records and observed other assessment tests that the school district requires, including Basic Reading Inventory and Observational Survey. In addition, I practiced Positive Behavior Support throughout my teaching experiences for all students and created an original unit called "Wild about Weather," taught with technology whenever possible; additionally, I wrote original poetry, songs and a children's book to enhance my lessons (to view: *www.goode.portfolio.net*).

My cooperating teacher and I attended an educational workshop on Response to Intervention (RtI). This reinforced my own teaching philosophy—every child has a unique set of strengths and needs; therefore, a teacher cannot assume that students are all on the same level at any one given time. I have been able to apply this knowledge by working closely with students on IEP's, including a boy with autism in our class, which was a remarkable experience. Overall, throughout all of my teaching experiences, I focused my teaching objectives on the diverse learning styles of children including differentiated learning and balanced literacy.

I am ready to use my strengths and talents to offer students the best education possible. That being said, I continue to enhance my skills by taking additional language and literacy seminars. My education, coupled with my teaching experiences has more than prepared me for the openings at Central Elementary, particularly my experience working with multi-age classrooms that align well with Central's Basic School philosophy. I am very interested in meeting with you at your convenience, and I want to thank you for your time and consideration. My résumé and application were submitted online as requested on your website. I look forward to hearing from you.

Sincerely,

put your signature here

Vera E. Goode

ONE MORE THING

If you really want to set yourself apart from other job seekers, you'll write a follow-up thank you letter after your interview. Seems like a no-brainer, right? Well, frankly, most candidates skip this opportunity to make a last ditch professional impression. Here's the scenario: *You've been invited to interview at a school district, you've had a good experience, and now you are at home waiting to hear about a second round of interviews or even a contract offer.* Use this last opportunity to thank the employer for the opportunity to interview, for the opportunity to meet the teaching team, and for the opportunity to learn more about the teaching position. Your follow-up thank you letter demonstrates your interest in the job and also demonstrates a basic courtesy—thanking someone who has invited you to a special occasion. You can send the letter as a pdf attachment to your email, or you can send it through the mail. Remember to be professional however you send it. Follow conventional letter writing guidelines.

TIP

Follow-up letters demonstrate basic courtesy and, at some level, a sense of sophistication. Employers pick up on this quickly. Don't miss this small, final step in Letter Writing 101.

The follow-up letter is a two to three paragraph letter that demonstrates your appreciation for the interview opportunity, reiterates your interest in the position, and basically keeps your name and face in front of the employer.

The following example leaves no doubt in the reader's mind about your interest in the job.

I would like to express my continued interest in the elementary position and the also express my appreciation for the courtesy and consideration I received during my interview and school tour at Central Elementary on the morning of March 18, 201x. As we discussed during our interview session, and throughout the tour, I feel I can contribute to the teaching team by sharing my collaborative approach, management techniques, and special reading and assessment skills. And, may I mention, that I am extremely excited about the energy I felt in the building and the enthusiasm of each person with whom I spoke.

My philosophy and specialized training fit nicely with Central's mission, curricula, and belief that every child can learn. I found the commitment of your staff most notable and would feel very comfortable being part of the primary team. As you know, the various field experiences through the University's teacher education program have afforded me with opportunities to gain experience in many facets of the school environment, including curriculum work, classroom procedures and management, as well as being involved in parent meetings, school carnivals, staff in-service, conferences and student productions of several types.

Please feel free to examine my online portfolio at www. goode.portfolio.net as well as the résumé and portfolio artifacts I left with you during my interview. I look forward to all future communication with you and your school district and please continue to consider me for this teaching position in your highly-regarded schools.

66 *I appreciate it when someone goes to that extra effort after the interview. It's one of those intangible things that can add something subtle and positive to my overall impression of you.* **99**

—Ross Wilburn, Equity Director and Central Office Administrator

It takes no more than 10 minutes to write a follow-up letter. Isn't 10 minutes worth the chance to get that perfect job? It's painless, and perhaps, the one small item that sets you apart from the other top candidates.

SUMMARY

Letters and Employer Communication

Cover letters and other forms of employer communication are a standard part of the job search process. Your professional correspondence catches the attention of employers and separates the best candidates from the rest. Strive for professionalism in all your communications. Your writing must have a purpose, but it must also give your candidacy sense and voice. Tell us a story—one that's interesting, unique and based on your experiences. The following activities can help.

ON THE WEB

ePlanner Activities

1. *My Letter Builder:* Building a better letter with three parts.
2. *Letter Sample and Template.*
3. *My Weekly Summary:* Find inspiration for your letters in your weekly overview.

eJournal

1. Observe your classroom/school environment and have a conversation with your classroom teacher about the design and function behind the classroom space. Why did your cooperating teacher decide to set up student desks or tables the way they are? What about the posters on the wall? What did you learn from this conversation?

PART 9

Interview Portfolios

"The job seeker without a portfolio is at a bit of a disadvantage. Let's look at candidate x and candidate y—one has a portfolio and the other doesn't. Candidate x shows me examples of collaborative projects, lesson plans, leadership experiences, multilingual proficiency, and technology skills . . . it doesn't take long to see why one has an advantage over the other."

—Dr. Jake Chung, Principal

My To-Do List

1. Select teaching artifacts that are professional and demonstrate your knowledge of standards.
2. Describe teaching artifacts to highlight key features and your strengths.
3. Learn how to effectively market yourself using a digital and paper-based Interview Portfolio.

My Project Overview

1. Take 5: Employer Role Play
2. My ePlanner
   Build My Interview Portfolio: Self promotion and job marketing through the following:
   a. Interview Portfolio Cover Page
   b. INTASC Standards
   c. Teaching Philosophy
   d. My Best Lesson Plan
   e. Classroom Management
   f. Differentiated Instruction
   g. Technology Integration
   h. Assessing Student Learning
   i. My Learning Environment Blueprint
   j. Student Teaching Reflections
   My Weekly Summary: Review your week in the classroom.
3. Take 5 Again: Practice with the Portfolio

Regardless of your teaching field or level—from early childhood to advanced placement secondary content—Interview Portfolios can document skills, showcase achievement and awards, highlight specialized training, demonstrate technology skills, and define aptitudes and attitudes. In other words, portfolios can tip the scales for job seekers by providing hard evidence to employers, validating interview answers, and exhibiting initiative. Putting together a portfolio helps you analyze who you are and what you have to offer to the workplace. That makes it great preparation for the interview.

TAKE 5

Employer Role Play

If you were making a staffing decision as a principal or head of the interview team, what evidence would you like to see of a teaching philosophy; classroom management; student success? Take 5 minutes to think about ways job seekers could demonstrate effectiveness in these key areas.

Portfolios have long been used in teacher preparation—some colleges and programs use a paper-based portfolio and some use digital portfolios—sometimes called ePortfolios, eFolios, or web portfolios. Whether paper-based or digital, they focus the spotlight on you and away from the competition. A portfolio's benefit isn't limited to the tremendous boost in employer enthusiasm for the tool. It also serves as an archive or vault of your professional work as an emerging teacher. Hey—it's all in your Portfolio. If you're worried that your teacher preparation program may not utilize ePortfolios—don't sweat it, because in this part, we're going to show you how to build an Interview Portfolio and partner it with artifacts from your teaching to put together a powerful job-seeking tool.

WHAT'S A PORTFOLIO ANYWAY?

Portfolio assessment goes with teacher education like butter goes with popcorn. For that reason, you've probably already got some sort of portfolio . . . the trick now is turning that into an Interview Portfolio. Nowadays, portfolios in education are almost exclusively tied to INTASC (Interstate New Teacher Assessment and Support Consortium Standards) or standards that are derived from the INTASC standards. Several teacher preparation programs have additional standards that relate to the particular strengths of that college. The standards dictate benchmarks for teacher performance, and surely your teacher preparation program has addressed these standards to some degree. We're not going to go into too much detail about the standards but rather focus our energy on how you can demonstrate teacher performances that are highly desirable by recruiters. For more information on the standards, view INTASC Standards in the web component. Standards-based portfolios are tools to present one's attainment of specified goals. Whether electronic or paper-based, portfolios that are organized around standards are often collections of artifacts that represent each or multiple standards.

ARTIFACT SELECTION

Artifacts are representations or examples of your work as an emerging teacher that reflect the goals and outcomes specified by the particular standard(s) that guided its selection. The best types of artifacts to include in your portfolio are those that demonstrate your mastery of teaching standards. In other words, the artifacts that you select should be polished, relevant, detailed, and convincing. Still struggling to understand what an artifact is? Most of you probably first heard the term *artifact* in the Indiana Jones movies—Dr. Jones goes hunting for ancient artifacts or relics of past civilizations. These artifacts represent something that is or was—a way of being and something that has meaning beyond itself. Think of an ancient clay pot. The pot wasn't just a pot—it was a vessel for carrying water, making food, and sometimes used for ceremonial purposes. The point is, the clay pot, much like a lesson plan, represents purpose and function. Take a look at the list of possible teacher artifacts that follows—think you don't have any? We bet you do.

100 POSSIBLE TEACHING ARTIFACTS

academic work samples
action plans
action research project
adaptations/differentiated
  learning strategies
administrative items of
  support
age-appropriate materials
anecdotal records
assessment instruments
assessment results
audio: Spanish; music
awards
behavior management
  plans
block scheduling example
booklists for students
case study
class lecture notes
classroom environment
  documentation
classroom management
  plans
classroom observation
  notes/reflections
classroom activities
coaching philosophy
coaching activities and record
collaborative projects
commendations
committee participation
communication samples
community service record
course syllabi
course descriptions
credentials
curriculum
documentation of meeting
  standards
educational certificates
employment record
evaluations (cooperating
  teacher/supervisor)
external assessments (state/
  national scores)
extra-duty activities

feedback
grading philosophy
goals/objectives
grading records/rubrics
grant writing sample
honors
inservice documentation
Individual Service Plans
innovative class projects
integrated instruction
  example
internal assessments
interdisciplinary teaching
  examples
interventions
instructional strategies
  (cooperative learning,
  discovery learning, direct
  instruction)
lab/technical reports
learning logs
lessons plans
lesson plan adaptations
letters of appreciation
licensure documents
long-term goals
memberships
military service
  documentation
multi-media samples
narrative report cards
newsletters
notes from meetings
observation feedback
parent communications
parent surveys
parent-teacher meeting
  documentation
performance evaluations
personal career statement
philosophy statement
planning materials
press releases
presentations
professional growth plan
professional development

projects showing
  diversity, inclusion/
  multiculturalism
public mention in media
published work
reading list (professional
  materials)
reading philosophy
report cards/grading
  rubrics
résumé
scholarship documentation
second-language evidence
self-evaluation statements
self-reflection in journal
short-term goals
snapshots of projects
standardized test scores
  comparison
student portfolio sample
student writing
student artifacts/student
  work
study guide(s)
summative appraisals
teacher journal
teaching philosophy
teaching awards
team-planning minutes
team-teaching project
technology competencies
  (hardware/software)
technology integration in
  lesson plans
technology philosophy
unit plan aligned to
  standards
units of instruction
unsolicited letters from
  parents, staff, colleagues
video segment—teaching
web-based projects
whole-class profiles
writing samples
website built by class
writing abstract

INAPPROPRIATE ARTIFACTS

Hiring officials must follow state and federal mandates. Inappropriate pre-employment information contained in portfolios may put potential employers at risk. Look at the following inappropriate artifacts:

- Photographs of friends, family, pets.
- Personal details—age, race, religion, marital status, dependents, partners.
- Political or religious affiliations.
- Tasteless or insensitive material.
- Inflammatory or derogatory statements about your placement, cooperating teachers, university supervisor and especially students.
- Be aware of issues of student confidentiality, photo or video releases or permissions.
- Copyrighted material that is not appropriately identified.

Some items above are probably included on your Facebook or Myspace page but never include these sorts of personal items in a portfolio—especially web-based versions. Employers want to hire teachers who understand professional context.

TIP

Irrelevant portfolio artifacts waste valuable interview time. Employers want to hire well-qualified people. Seeing a picture of your cat won't help facilitate a job offer.

VALUE OF PORTFOLIOS

Portfolios are valuable for two reasons: for students they are an active archive and framework that supports continued growth and development as a teacher, and for employers they provide evidence of ability, a clear picture of your identity, and proof of your credentials. Little time need be wasted in the first critical minutes of the interview. Employers can cut to the chase and talk about key items included in your portfolio. In other words, employers can get beyond blue shirts and white shirts, the striped tie or no tie, and get down to business about what you can bring to this job. For both parties, portfolios are an effective way to demonstrate standards based legitimacy. Portfolios are also an excellent tool for job seekers to synthesize coursework, field experience, and student teaching to prepare for the interview. Not to mention, most early career teachers have to demonstrate their abilities as a teacher during annual performance reviews. Portfolio assessment is a skill that every new teacher needs to possess. Why not get a head start, and a leg up on the competition, by putting together an Interview Portfolio?

INTERVIEW PORTFOLIO

Building a standards-based Interview Portfolio is easier than it sounds, and the return on the investment is great. If you are enrolled in a program that utilizes a web-based ePortfolio you're already half-way there. In fact, your program may already encourage the use of your ePortfolio in the employment process—even better. Follow your program guidelines and recommendations for providing employer access to your ePortfolio site. If your ePortfolio isn't web based or is password protected you may want to download artifacts and burn to a CD or USB flash drive. You can then provide employers copies of your ePortfolio on a CD or USB flash drive, or share a Dropbox link. USB flash drives are a cheap and efficient way to provide the rich benefit your ePortfolio adds to the application process. Consider really putting yourself online by uploading your ePortfolio to the web. Many colleges and universities offer students free web space to do just that. Check in with your campus technology center to see if that's an option for you.

If your teacher preparation program uses a paper-based assessment portfolio, don't sweat it, because chances are, your portfolio artifacts are saved electronically on your USB flash drive or computer hard drive. That's all you'll need to get started on building an Interview Portfolio that you can share as a paper-copy or as an electronic file with employers—heck, you too can have an ePortfolio! Keep reading.

BUILDING MY INTERVIEW PORTFOLIO

Throughout the first eight parts of "Getting Hired," we've given you focused reflection prompts through the eJournal, ePlanner, and Take 5 activities. We've also encouraged you to consider specific examples from your own experiences. Each time, we've indicated that we'd get to this in Part 9; well, here we are. It's time to put those building blocks together into a powerful interview tool: your Interview Portfolio (IP). Your IP will be composed of several templates that are downloadable from the Getting Hired website. You'll customize each of these templates and add your own unique experiences to paint a rich picture of you as an emerging practitioner.

Your IP is a versatile job-seeking tool. Because the templates are electronic files you have a couple of presentation options. You can customize and print a paper-based IP to share with employers. You can also save all the documents together in either Microsoft Word or Adobe pdf format and share with employers electronically as an email attachment or application upload. Even if you choose to share your IP with employers electronically, you'll still want to make sure you take a paper copy of it to a job fair or interview. It's a great tool to reference while answering an interview question, and your IP demonstrates comprehensive and thorough preparation. And what employer doesn't want a thoroughly prepared and sincere new teacher? Not every candidate goes through all that work! Your IP will be most effective if you have artifacts associated with it—either summarized in the templates provided, or as inserts following the templates pages. So for example, the IP template, My Best Lesson Plan, might be followed by your actual lesson plan. Likewise, Assessing Student Learning might be followed by an assessment rubric, quiz, or summative assessment you developed while head teaching. This assessment might even be related to My Best Lesson Plan, painting an even richer picture of that particular unit during student teaching.

Think you can do it? We know you can! *Here's what you'll need:*

- eJournals,
- "Take 5" questions,
- ePlanner assignments,
- Getting Hired website in order to download the Interview Portfolio Templates.

How This Works

When you log into the Getting Hired website you'll find the Interview Portfolio Templates. There is one downloadable PDF that contains 10 embedded templates. They are the following:

- **Interview Portfolio Cover Sheet**
  Add your name and teaching area above the table of contents. If you choose not to include a particular artifact page (listed below), be sure to delete it from the table of contents. This page introduces you.
- **INTASC Standards Page**
  The INTASC Standards page introduces the standards and directs employer's attention to the fact that your Interview Portfolio is standards-based. The Standards page is also a nice review for you and a potential cheat sheet during the interview should questions come up related to the standards.
- **Teaching Philosophy**
  You've already written about your teaching philosophy in a Take 5 and eJournal activities. Now copy your ideas and place them in an organized and professional manner into this IP template. Be ready to share how your philosophy will be evident in your classroom.
- **My Best Lesson Plan**
  Find your best lesson plan from student teaching and reflect on it here. Include a copy of your lesson plan with handouts or examples after this IP page.
- **Classroom Management**
  This is often the gatekeeper question for new teachers. Revisit your classroom management strategies and summarize them here. Share examples from student teaching.
- **Differentiated Instruction**
  We've encouraged you throughout the semester to get serious experience learning about meeting the needs of each learner. Now's your chance to share

that information with potential employers. Provide specific examples from your experience on how you have differentiated instruction to meet the needs of all learners in your classroom.

- **Technology Integration**
Teachers of the future need to be able to demonstrate effective means of technology integration and technology literacy. How do you integrate technology to support learning and student achievement? Which tools do you use to promote student learning and motivation?

- **Assessing Student Learning**
Formal and informal assessment is a topic at every interview. Share examples of how you make decisions, assess student learning, and adjust your teaching to meet the needs of students.

- **My Learning Environment Blueprint**
Employers are always curious about what your classroom might look like and how you design your room to maximize student success. Share how you make these decisions.

- **Student Teaching Reflections**
Student teaching often forms the basis of most interview questions and is the launch pad of a successful career in teaching. Pull examples from your Weekly Summaries—they're a great resource to reflect on the big picture. Revisit the 10 truths of student teaching to demonstrate how you've grown and become a relationship builder and a reflective practitioner.

It might seem like an overwhelming task, but remember—most of these artifacts are already saved in one form or another on your hard drive. All teacher preparation programs address these core issues with emerging teachers, so think back to your coursework, haul out those eJournals, and reread your answers to the Take 5 questions throughout Getting Hired. You'll have plenty to write about.

Here are a few more tips as you develop your Interview Portfolio:

- Presentation is key, both in terms of visual appeal and your content. We've created templates that we know look good—so don't ruin them by adding fonts above size 10. Stick with simple common fonts (no Jokerman please), and avoid excessive bold, italics, or other such clutter.
- Keep it professional—remember you want to communicate professionalism even if your best lesson plan was about earthworms! Make sure that the information presented highlights your skills as a teacher, your attention to student learning, and awareness of content and curriculum.
- Proof! Or all you've proven is that you're not able to pay attention to detail. Reading thousands of résumés gives HR directors an uncanny ability to find typos . . . and they report to us that's the number one way to get kicked out of consideration! Remember, as a teacher, you're teaching kids how to spell correctly and do good work.

- Be specific and direct. Avoid verbal diarrhea—you know the kind of story that goes on and on without any control or end. For example, include a lesson plan but not a unit plan. You want to make sure the reader doesn't lose interest in you. Make every page count; make every item count. Always, though, select the best, most convincing, and most current items that highlight the abilities most desired in your teaching specialty.
- If you string the templates together in a single word or pdf document—make sure you test the document by sending it to yourself and opening and viewing all pages. Sometimes formatting is lost and again, failure to proof and double check could mean the difference in getting hired.

TIP

"Portfolios provide talking points during the interview. Portfolio artifacts provide demonstrated evidence of what you've done. It's another way to sell yourself—it's a valuable thing to have."

—Jim Pedersen, Executive Director of Human Resources

It's easy to see how candidates who share their Interview Portfolio with potential employers have made lasting positive first impressions by substantiating their credentials with solid examples of their performance as emerging teachers. An Interview Portfolio communicates sincerity and interest in self-improvement, attention to detail in reflection, and true professionalism. Selecting the right person for the job is one of the most important functions of a hiring official. Portfolios give employers more tools, evidence, and examples that can help prove that you have the right stuff for their job.

THE INTERVIEW PORTFOLIO DURING THE INTERVIEW

The very nature of Interview Portfolios can provide you versatility and control over the job-seeking process that other parts of the application process can't. Most of you will fill out online or paper-based application materials where you'll list things like coursework, volunteer experiences, job experiences. Why not bring those boring lists to life by showcasing course projects, papers, and work-related projects? Turn being a volunteer at a neighborhood youth center into being a life changer— someone making real differences in kids' lives. You can do it in your Interview Portfolio in ways that aren't available on applications or résumés. Your IP could contain artifacts about volunteering, including video of your awe-inspiring work, images of the programs you organized, testimonials about your impact. Because your IP can be web-based, why not link to videos or other media you've uploaded to YouTube, or other free web hosting tools? We're pretty sure that most of you are pretty tech savvy—think about utilizing all the wonderful web tools available nowadays as you begin to market yourself.

If you choose to share your IP with an employer ahead of time, you'd be surprised how the nature of questioning changes. Because they've already viewed your artifacts and customized IP templates, the questions might be more specific, more detailed, and more based on your experiences. How easy is that? Rather than asking you to talk about your interactions with parents, an employer who's already seen samples of parent communications in a portfolio might ask about a specific letter you wrote, or what the result of your communication was. Open-ended "nebulous" questions are always harder to answer than targeted, detailed, you-centered questions. But we offer one caution—employers want to use interview time wisely, and some will welcome your references to your Interview Portfolio and entertain your willingness to share and others may prefer to not view that during the interview. Some districts have structured protocols, so don't be offended if they decline your Interview Portfolio. Understand and remember that the value isn't just in the employer's take on the tool, but in the reflection, attention to detail, and practice that you got while assembling it.

TAKE 5 **AGAIN**

Practice with the Portfolio

Print your Interview Portfolio. Once your Interview Portfolio is assembled, imagine you're sitting across the table from an employer who asks: "Why should I hire you?" Using your Interview Portfolio as a guide, convince the employer that you have a commitment to student learning and student success, as evidenced by the artifacts you've included. Have something definitive to say about each of your artifacts. Jot down your notes here.

SUMMARY

Interview Portfolios

Assembling an Interview Portfolio is probably the best possible practice for an interview. The next phase of this book deals exactly with that—interview preparations. Your Interview Portfolio represents you, and if you aren't yet an expert on you, your Interview Portfolio will help. Employers expect to hear about each of the topics in your IP. Employers also want to know that you are familiar with standards—and each piece of your IP addresses one or more of the INTASC standards. Your IP is documentation that you are a professional. It's time to put it all together, and the following activities will help.

ON THE WEB

ePlanner Activities

1. *Build My Interview Portfolio:* Self promotion and job marketing through the following:
   a. Interview Portfolio Cover Page
   b. INTASC Standards
   c. Teaching Philosophy
   d. My Best Lesson Plan
   e. Classroom Management
   f. Differentiated Instruction
   g. Technology Integration
   h. Assessing Student Learning
   i. My Learning Environment Blueprint
   j. Student Teaching Reflections
2. *My Weekly Summary:* Review your week in the classroom.

eJournal

1. Once you've assembled an Interview Portfolio, in what ways do you feel more confident or better prepared for the interview? How do your artifacts interface with the standards?

PHASE 3

Getting Hired

Getting hired. Most of you probably can't believe that you're just a few short weeks away from completing your teacher preparation program. Some of you have already attended job fairs, had interviews, and made strong job contacts. Hopefully, some of you even have contracts in hand, or are well on your way. Getting hired is a mindset— knowing you have what an employer is looking for and an ability to articulate it effectively. Get hired—you know that you're ready for this.

The job search never happens at a good time, and at the penning of this page, the Great Recession is officially over, but unemployment remains a problem. The craziness of student teaching coupled with a challenging job market make it easy to lose hope and feel as though despite your greatest efforts, your job options are bleak. Guess what—that couldn't be any further from the truth, because unless every student teacher buys this book, you've got a great advantage. You've been thinking about what makes a great teacher since page one. You've been encouraged to reflect on your strengths and build tools that will promote and provide evidence of professionalism and a high standard of quality that many candidates will lack. Get hired—you really are an excellent candidate armed with the tools, the tips, and insider knowledge you'll need to get an employer's attention.

The last phase of this book is about the interview. You've done everything you can to get there. Why blow it now? You've already spent a great deal of time preparing for the interview—even if it seems the only thing you've been doing is trying to keep your head above water. There are many venues in which you may encounter an employer—be prepared in each. Time to turn that professionalism up a notch, because in this home stretch all eyes are on you. We share tips for interviewing and the most common interview questions. Employers are looking for one thing in your answers—evidence of student success. You are a good teacher, because you know how and why your students learn. More importantly, you care that they learn. It's time to get hired.

PART 10

Interview Preparations

Dr. Jake Chung, Principal, says: "Nothing beats a well prepared candidate during an interview. Don't forget that we'll likely have other people to interview so it's you against others. We look for preparation, attention to detail, body language, and fit. The interview process works."

My To-Do List

1. Understand the expectations and etiquette of different interview settings.
2. Dress for success—interview attire that will seal the deal.
3. Do your homework—interview research that will give you a leg up on the competition.

My Project Overview

1. Take 5: Mirror Mirror on the Wall, Who's the Best Candidate of All?
2. My ePlanner
   a. *My Research about the Job:* What I know, what I need to know.
   b. *My Job-Seeking References:* Folks whom I can use during the job search.
   c. *Interview Dates and Details:* Know the details, get hired.
   d. *My Weekly Summary:* Keeping it real in the final stretch.
3. Take 5 Again: Time to Get Ready—Time to Get Hired

Have you ever wondered if those videos that promise perfectly sculpted bodies in just minutes a day are real? In fact, some promise those effects in just 10 minutes a day. What if we told you that just 10 minutes a day, every day, during your student teaching could do the same thing for your image as a teacher? Uh, sorry, we're not talking about the way you look. We're talking about the way you sound, the way you come off, and the way you present yourself as the next best thing to happen in education when you meet with employers during the interview process. That's right, in just 10 minutes a day you, too, can transform your image, tighten your absolutely fantastic answers to interview questions, firm up your but-ever-so-terrific teaching philosophy, and trim your waste-of-time, go-nowhere interview answers. Give 10 minutes to a new interview you!

TAKE 5

Mirror Mirror on the Wall, Who's the Best Candidate of All?

Get a mirror! That's right, get a mirror and practice:

Meeting someone for the first time. Walk up with your hand stretched out and a big smile. How do you look? Inviting?

Your 30-second "All about me" spiel.

Answering a question you've prepared. Think about eye contact. Smile with your eyes and mannerisms.

All of the above works for face-to-face, phone, and web-based interviews.

Get a roommate, friend, parent! Once you're convinced you're ready to take your show on the road, practice with some live bait. Practice introducing yourself to your roommates, parents, friends. Tell them about yourself. Thank them for offering to interview you. Have them ask a question or two.

When you're done, ask them if you did anything weird, like fidget, shake your leg, not make eye contact. It's a fun way to practice for the real interview.

GET READY TO GET HIRED

Since you've spent the time to draft a convincing cover letter and coherent résumé, don't blow it all by being underprepared for the interview. The fact is, too many candidates think that getting the interview is the hard part. Wrong! Getting the job is the hard part and that includes having a successful interview.

Here's the skinny—pun intended! Too many new teachers are overconfident in their abilities to deliver a knock-'em-dead type of interview. Why? Chances are it has something to do with the very nature of student teaching. By the time most of you get to the interviewing stage, student teaching will be well underway, if not nearly over. You've garnered a tremendous amount of experience in that period of time and have *plenty* to talk about. You've had to turn in a reflection on just about everything and you've had conversations about every topic known to teaching. You feel like a pro. Then the interview arrives. You walk in feeling like a rockstar and leave feeling dumber than a rock. How could you not think of anything you'd done when they asked about differentiation? Why did you tell *that* story when you were asked about a conflict you'd resolved? You didn't mean to badmouth your cooperating teacher but realized you inadvertently had. Forget about the standards because you did! Yep, sad but true, frankly more people blow it during the interview than are successful. So, here's the deal. If you give yourself 10 minutes a day from the first day of student teaching, you'll be ready to rock *and* roll at your interviews.

UNDERSTANDING INTERVIEW SETTINGS

You'll never know where it will happen. And, sometimes you won't even know it's happening. You are in line at the grocery store and suddenly the person waiting behind you strikes up a conversation about the price of food these days. You return with a funny quip. A conversation starts . . . in the course of the conversation you mention that you are student teaching at the neighborhood school. You are asked if you enjoy your work, if you find it challenging and rewarding, and of course your answers are all positive. Thank goodness because you have just met the superintendent in the grocery line! After you pay, the superintendent asks your permission to contact your cooperating teacher and implies that you might want to apply online if interested. There you go. You just had your first interview.

We are not suggesting that you make excessive trips to the grocery store. We are suggesting, however, that you be ready for a variety of interview settings. Some are in person in a school building or a campus job fair. Others are over the phone or Internet. Some happen in the most random and unexpected places—some are planned, some are impromptu, some are scheduled, some are spontaneous. Be ready to sound and look the part regardless whether it's in cyberspace or in a real place. Each setting requires a bit of specific preparation. Let's review the most common types of interviews and how to prepare for them.

The Job Fair

Job fairs are a great way to meet recruiters and make serious job connections. Your college or university program might host or partner in hosting a job fair. Job fairs are typically half-day or full-day recruiting events depending on the size of the fair. Some job fairs have hundreds of districts in attendance while others are more intimate with fewer than 10 districts in attendance. Whatever the size—get there early and plan to stay as long as you can. A job fair is a great way to put a face with the résumé—to stand out among the masses. Here are a few sure fire tips to make your trip to the job fair a success:

1. Get suited up—to get hired. Unfortunately, too many candidates don't take job fairs seriously and show up in boring khakis. Stand out, suit up, and you'll be sure to wow recruiters with your serious professionalism and appearance.
2. Talk to as many schools, recruiters, and candidates as you can. Spend the entire fair networking. Even if your dream job is only in one district—talk to as many districts as you can. You never know whom you'll meet and whom they can help you meet. Too many candidates leave early from job fairs and miss out on great opportunities by not meeting as many districts as possible.

Even if they're not looking for teachers in your area at that time, they might take note of the great candidate (you) they met at a job fair, and call you later in the hiring season.

3. Take plenty of résumés. You've grown up in a generation that really makes you feel guilty for excess printing and, well, they're right, but just resolve to do one less worksheet with your classes once you become a teacher. Print extra copies of your résumé. Some schools bring more than one recruiter! Have some backups ready to go.

   Take a few copies of your Interview Portfolio: You've spent a great deal of time preparing the portfolio, which in turn has better prepared you to quickly talk about your strengths as a potential hire. Offer your Interview Portfolio as an example of your work. If an employer decides to keep it, don't worry—you can print out another one.

4. Pay close attention to announcements of job fairs—some require advance registration, charge a fee, and even have scheduled interviews. Make the most of your opportunity by paying attention to the details. Register early and try to sign up for interviews if possible.

5. Do your homework—know who'll be in attendance and look for any added information or employment details. Know as much as you can about a district—this preparation really pays off, and employers can tell when candidates have done their homework.

6. Make an impression, not a statement. Obnoxious attention-seeking behavior is never recommended. Even if you're trying to stand out among 2,000+ job seekers—save the chicken suit for the county fair—not the job fair.

7. Be well rested and nourished before the fair. Some larger job fairs typically have long lines—and waits. Be prepared to do a lot of standing—look fresh and well polished by staying alert and in good spirits in the lines . . . recruiters are watching you. Smile, Smile, Smile.

8. Send a follow-up email to recruiters after the job fair thanking them for the opportunity to visit about their district and reiterate your interest in working for them.

Hop online and locate a job fair in your area. It's an excellent opportunity to meet recruiters and practice your interviewing skills. Job fair interviews are typically short 5–15 minute conversations. Make sure you've practiced some power-packed succinct statements so you can best utilize the short amount of time you have to make a great connection.

Phone Interviews

Phone interviews are becoming more common because it's a relatively inexpensive way to conduct initial screening of candidates shortlisted for interviews. Most districts can only realistically interview three to five candidates for each position so phone interviews are a great way to whittle down the pool of applicants invited to campus for interviews. Here are a few phone interview tips:

1. Give a phone number that employers can use to reach you. This may or may not be the phone number they have from your résumé. Make sure you confirm the phone number they plan to call.

2. Confirm other details too like time of call, approximate duration, whether it will be a conference call and, if so, with whom you'll be speaking.

3. If you've provided a cell number, make sure your batteries are charged and you're in an area where you get good reception.

4. Plan for privacy. Privacy—make sure you're not going to worry if a roommate can hear your conversation. Avoid any potential distractions by arranging the call at a time when you won't have to worry about or deal with others. Don't take the phone call while at your student teaching site—that's just unprofessional. Schedule the interview at a time that is convenient for your teaching responsibilities.

5. A phone interview is still a real interview—dress up, they won't be able to see it, but they'll sure hear the added bonus. Looking like a professional adds to any professional conversation, and be prepared as if you're visiting campus.

6. Thank them at the beginning and at the end of the conversation. Since they won't be able to see what a professional you are, you'll have to make an extra effort to sound professional. Be enthusiastic on the phone.

7. Have all your materials at your fingertips. Use your résumé, portfolio, and other materials to reference specific examples.

Phone interviews are a great way for most candidates to show their interpersonal skills. Be prepared to have a great conversation—you'll be happy you did.

Voice Message

Telephone rings . . . Ring . . . Ring . . . Ring:

Voice Message Service: *Heeeeey! It's Lisa . . . I'm either dancing on a table, or under the table! If you're calling me about last night I plead the fifth because I don't remember. If you're calling about last weekend, we're cool . . . OK, leave a message unless it's you, dad—I'm kidding around.*

Voice on the other end: *Uhhhh, hi Lisa, this is Bob Smith the, uhhhh, Principal at Springfield Elementary, uhhhh just calling to see if you'd be available for an interv . . . ooops you know what . . . I think I have the wrong number.*
Click.

Don't blow your chances of getting hired by forgetting to make sure that your professional presence reaches all the areas an employer might "reach." Candidates often forget to make sure that voice mail or answering machine messages are professional sounding. Why lose a job, or a potential interview, because an employer was turned off by an unprofessional phone or voice message? Likewise, if you have roommates, be sure to have a discussion with them about taking messages from potential employers. Encourage roommates not to disclose any personal information when taking a message, but to be professional, thank them for calling, and assure them that the message to return the call will reach you as soon as possible. Make sure your cell phone is able to take a message (namely, that your inbox isn't too full—recruiters comment that this happens more than we'd like it to), and remember to have a warm professional greeting. Take a look at the wrong and the right kind of phone message:

> **Wrong:**
> Heeeey! What's up? You've reached Lisa's cell phone. I'm not able to take your call, so leave a message. TTYL!

> **Right:**
> Hi. You've reached the cell phone of Lisa Smith. I'm not available right now, but please leave a message and your phone number and I'll get back to you as soon as possible. Thank you.

Likewise, phone messages with background music, special effects, or otherwise immature and impolite overtones should all be avoided. In the end, the small details related to professional etiquette can have big effects on your career.

Web-based Interviews

The use of web-based video conferencing tools to screen candidates at a distance will likely continue to grow in popularity as the interface becomes more ubiquitous. Most new computer systems come with all the necessary tools built in. Web-based video conferencing is a wonderful way to meet employers and demonstrate professionalism—not to mention technology prowess in this day and age. From Skype to social media enabled video chat, there are multiple platforms that facilitate this interaction. Candidates should familiarize themselves with the tool—be it Skype or some other service. Quality of service is sometimes an issue in areas with less broadband access. Most service providers include operational requirements on their websites that can test an individual's system. If your computer isn't an option—check with your college or university to see if there are facilities available that might work. Don't forget that you'll have to create a user account and share your User ID with the potential employer. You might find this tool so useful that you meet with your university supervisor to discuss your placement over the web-based service. Here are a few more tips before you log in for a web-based interview:

1. Be sure to dress up—don't forget they can see you!
2. If you're doing this at home, don't forget to be aware of your surroundings. Do you really want an employer to see the four weeks of dishes or laundry you've been neglecting? If you're doing it on campus—find a location that affords you some privacy and quiet.

3. Log in ahead of time—practice with the software and interface. Have a friend or peer from your seminar class practice with you. It takes a while to get used to talking to your computer!

4. Remember to make "eye contact" by looking at the camera. Avoid staring at yourself (sometimes available in a small window) you'll be distracted and probably fuss over things you wouldn't otherwise even notice.

5. Smile, smile, smile. There's nothing more taxing on our poor brains than talking to an inanimate object like the computer. Just remember to smile, it makes the whole ordeal seem less bizarre. Try to show a sense of humor, too—laughter is a good thing.

6. Log on before the interview to position the camera and check the sound. Make sure you're logged out and the camera isn't rolling after the interview.

❝We had just finished a Skype interview and the candidate thought he had logged out when all he had done was turn the camera off—we could still hear him and boy did he have some unpleasant things to say about how the interview went. Needless to say in our rejection letter we were sure to mention that he had been our top contender for the job until that mishap.❞

—Comments from a School HR Conference

It's certainly recommended that candidates familiarize themselves with the interface ahead of time. Getting used to looking at a camera and articulating for the microphone all while looking at a computer screen may seem strange until you practice it a bit.

Dress for Success

You've been impressing all the folks with your professional dress and demeanor during student teaching. Now it's time to step up your game a notch by dressing for the interview. What's the costume for an interview? A suit, of course. That's right. Put away the khakis because they're just too informal for an all-out interview. We haven't asked you to buy anything yet, have we? Hope not, because you're going to be laying down some dough for this one. Professional and quality suiting is pricey and there simply isn't any way around it. We strongly recommend you buy the best possible suit you can afford. Here's why—a suit, like your college education, is something that usually offers a good return on your investment. For starters, it communicates professionalism, respect (for yourself and interviewers), and dignity. A suit tells the interview team you're serious about what you do and why you're there. It helps to build that first impression that's so important and singular. A quality suit in a standard and conservative color like black also can be used for just about every professional occasion. Need a different look for a second interview? Wear a different shirt and tie combo, or a differently colored blouse.

Trust us—what won't be noticed is that you're wearing the same suit—what will be noticed is that you're taking this seriously. That's a strong message to send.

All you need is one suit—one suit to make a great first impression—even if that happens 20 times before you land a job.

Additional Considerations When Purchasing a Suit

- Give yourself plenty of time to get a suit altered. A suit that fits just right has a certain wow-factor to it that gives you an indescribable advantage during the interview.
- Wool breathes better than polyester. Generally speaking, wool is the best fabric choice—but be reasonable, you don't want to turn anyone off by sweating through the interview either.
- Keep your suit pressed. Hang it up to air out after each wearing. Dry cleaning your suit is good occasionally, but remember the more you get it dry cleaned the sooner it begins to wear out. Generally speaking, hanging the suit to air out in a well ventilated area does the trick.
- A $2.00 fabric roller generally is a great investment when it comes to removing unwanted animal hair, lint, or dust.
- Don't ruin a good suit with poorly chosen accessories. In fact, it's a good idea to take the suit, or a piece of it, with you when you're shopping for accessories. If all else fails—ask the sales associate or clothier to assist you. It's why they're there.

Some Other Good Interview Advice

- Don't make drastic changes to your hair style before you interview—you'll spend too much time thinking about that. With that said, a good haircut never hurts.
- Keep any facial hair trimmed and groomed.
- Women should avoid excessive make-up; men should avoid make-up altogether.
- Body art (tattoos) and piercings should be covered or removed if they are beyond the ordinary, distracting, or if they look painful. Remember, you're working with kids! Anything that makes a non-pierced or tattooed individual say ouch or yikes should fall in this category. We don't mean to offend, we're just being honest!
- Shoes should be formal and be appropriate for the outfit. If you notice your feet during the interview you're paying attention to the wrong thing.
- Avoid cologne or perfume. Smell is one of our most powerful senses and has a direct link to our memory. You never know what past memories—good or bad—might be evoked by wearing certain scents. Get someone's attention with your smarts, not your scents.

Everything should look like it fits and is intentional. Your attention to your appearance speaks volumes to employers seeking to staff their classrooms. Seriously, it all boils down to looking well groomed—top to bottom. Administrators always think about two things with respect to your attire: what will s/he look like in front of parents, and is this person professional? If they don't feel good about the way you look—forget it. They'll move to the next candidate.

" *There have been far too many applicants who arrive at the interview in casual attire. An example would be the very capable candidate last week who arrived in khakis and a wrinkled blouse. The team could not look past the informality of her attire.***"**

—Cindi Diouf, Administrator

Do Your Homework

Administrators are looking for folks who've done their homework about the district before they arrive for an interview. Doing your research about the organization for which you're about to interview does you good during the interview, too. It informs your answers, and communicates intentionality and a sincere interest in working for a school.

We asked administrators what you should know about a school before the interview, and this is what they told us:

- *Know as much as possible about the specific position and the building:* That includes the school website, the curriculum, the grade level, the teaching team, the technology. Does the school have any unique programs. Is it a charter, magnet, K–5, K–8, K–3, ninth grade center, high school, junior high, or middle school? Do they have combined grades, a before/afterschool program, an active parent group? Drive by before the interview and check out the infrastructure, playground, sports facilities, and anything else that seems interesting.
- *Know the district:* Demographics, enrollments, growth, testing data, curriculum, what the school board is discussing. Drive by a few of the schools—are there multiple high schools? Middle schools or junior highs? What are you able to learn about their standards? Does the school district have a motto or mission that's interesting? Can you weave it into your teaching philosophy? Do they make school improvement plans available online? What's the school's track record in sports, academics, and extracurriculars?
- *Know the resources available for staff:* Most districts have a web page devoted to staff issues. See what's available there. Is there a professional development schedule? Information on benefits, salary, the negotiated contract? Some Human Resources offices post comprehensive information about the application process. Some districts intentionally post interview rubrics "for

administrators." Hello! That's a huge give-away. They're practically putting a one-way ticket to getting the job in your lap. Don't forgo the opportunity to learn whatever you can about a district's hiring procedures.

- *Know the community:* Size, demographics, issues, news, sports, layout . . . where are things located, what are the neighboring school districts? Are there school/community partnerships?

You could probably spend hours doing some "job-stalking" and that wouldn't necessarily be a bad thing. Some school and district websites on the other hand are easily traversed in their entirety in a matter of minutes. Do your best, and allocate as much time as you can to doing your homework about your future employer but don't forget to prepare answers to your interview questions too. Be certain that you're continuing to prioritize your time effectively to allow for continued successful student teaching.

Letters of Recommendation

Letters of recommendation continue to be a vital part of the screening and selection process. Your letters document academic training, professional abilities, scholastic achievement, and employment history, even if your employment history is limited to one semester of student teaching experience. Few educational employers can offer a contract without collecting letters of recommendation from reliable sources. In your case, reliable sources would include the following:

- Your cooperating teacher;
- Your university supervisor;
- Your faculty advisor;
- Your supervisor in a related work setting (with youth).

Note: No employer is interested in a letter from a friend, relative, or neighbor. These individuals cannot speak to your competence in your subject field. Obtain letters of recommendation from people with authoritative knowledge of or administrative responsibility for your education or employment. Evaluations/merit reviews, recommendations from students or parents of students, and character references are not appropriate for a professional job search.

The Unpredictable Nature of a Job Interview

Regardless of how well you prepare, though, interviews always have elements of unpredictability. There is always the chance that a random and unanticipated comment will be made or an unexpected question asked. Hopefully, your interview preparation will help you weather those unavoidable and uncontrollable moments like a pro, rather than leaving you feeling like you've just been ambushed. Employers do their best to help you feel at ease and comfortable, and they know you're nervous, but only you can control how well prepared you are to manage the stress of an interview.

Interviews = Stress

❝*Stress . . . stress . . . stress . . .*

Some candidates handle stress well.

Some candidates get nervous, wither, look uncomfortable.

Figure out how you react under stress.

By anticipating stress, you'll be better able to handle it.

KNOW YOURSELF!❞

—Ann Feldmann, Assistant Superintendent

TIP

Even if you're not a sports fan, this topic often comes up in casual conversation. It's never a bad idea to have something to say even if it's acknowledging that although you think you know the difference between the Cubs and the Bears, in Chicago say, that's about where your knowledge of the two teams stops. That's a potentially humorous way to dodge those kinds of questions. If you're not interviewing in Chicago, just replace those team names with whatever other professional or college teams might be there.

Why Not Be Over-prepared?

Why take the chance of going to an interview and being under-prepared? It's like walking into a final exam without reading the textbook or reviewing the class notes. It's like going to a really important engagement and arriving under-dressed. It's embarrassing and knocks you off-guard for a moment while you figure out what to do or what to say to the host. Most interview problems are like that as well. It's just that moment of indecision, that quick look of terror that can make others just a bit cautious to approach you with a welcoming hello.

TIP

Employers in stateside and international schools are surprised that they need to say this over and over:

"There is just no excuse for somebody who's interested in a job not to have gone online to check us out, to get a good background of what that school's all about. So, do your homework before you show up."

Lack of preparation seems to be the biggest problem for most job seekers. *Study* for the interview. *Research, review,* and be ready to *talk* about what you know.

Employers expect you to be ready for the interview. Why shouldn't they? You've spent hours creating good marketing tools, you've collected letters of recommendation, you've completed the school's application form, and now you've accepted an interview invitation. Employers anticipate you to be on your toes, to be prepared to talk about yourself and about the school and the community. Even though employers have encountered many job applicants who arrive ill-prepared, they are still surprised and perplexed when it happens.

COMMON INTERVIEW PROBLEMS

Every interview presents challenges and opportunities. Because most interviews initiate some feelings of inadequacy, missteps can be made in key interview areas including answering questions, nonverbal cues, and basic behavior. Employers bemoan the fact that many good applicants fall victim to preventable mistakes. Don't let any of *the Big 10* end your job chances.

INTERVIEW MISTAKES: THE BIG 10+1

The Big 10 + one

1. Inarticulate answers
2. Unable to identify strengths or weaknesses
3. Hadn't thought through "beliefs"
4. No clear sense of purpose
5. Insufficient research on school and community
6. Unorganized, unprepared for questions
7. Exaggerated abilities/arrogance
8. Unaware of national issues in education
9. Negative body language and lack of eye contact
10. Poor interpersonal skills
11. Inappropriate dress

Let's agree that all of these interview problems can be alleviated if you just take a few minutes and think about them. Resolve to go through each one and devise a plan so that an employer never thinks that you entered into a professional conversation, a professional job discussion, without a plan.

MISTAKE #1
Inarticulate Answers

Resolve to practice ahead of time—share with the mirror or with a friend or family member your beliefs about student learning in your subject area. If they tell you that you stutter and stammer and say "um" before each phrase listen to them and keep practicing.

MISTAKE #2
Unable to Identify Strengths and/or Weaknesses

Resolve to figure this out immediately before you accept another interview invitation. It's basic that you know what your strengths are in both your teaching area and in your general role as a school educator. Weaknesses should be just as easy to talk about. We all can learn more about technology, management strategies, and motivational techniques.

MISTAKE #3
Beliefs and Philosophy

Resolve to go back and carefully review your philosophy statement to determine your conviction about teaching and learning. Did you create a motto or mission statement? If not, now is a good time to visit the Interview Portfolio in Part 9 and complete your Teaching Philosophy. Employers want to hire people with passion, with confidence about their pedagogy, and with a well-grounded philosophy.

MISTAKE #4
No Clear Sense of Purpose

Resolve to take a few minutes with no distractions and think about your reasons for wanting to teach. Why did you choose this profession instead of another? What can you bring to this profession that will make a difference? Think, and then jot your ideas down because they will be useful as you answer even the most rudimentary interview question.

MISTAKE #5

Insufficient Research about School and Community

Resolve to Google . . . it's as simple as that. Every school has some type of web presence with basic information about their school, students, and staff. It's the easiest thing you can do and one of the most important. Just do it!

MISTAKE #6

Unorganized and Unprepared for Questions

Resolve to take the interview appointment very seriously. Employers and search teams are very busy and have put significant duties aside to meet with you in a professional setting. To have someone show up for an important meeting and then be ill-equipped to respond to inquiries is a big disappointment.

MISTAKE #7

Exaggerated Abilities/Arrogance

Resolve to think before you talk. Sounds easy but apparently it's not. Just tell the employer what you have done and don't waste time or energy embellishing your grades or your teaching talents. Because hiring officials interview hundreds, even thousands of people, they have a good sense of who is telling the truth—much like a police officer.

MISTAKE #8

Unaware of National Issues in Education

Resolve to pick up a newspaper or go on the Internet and you'll see any number of issues that employers will want to hear about: poverty, dropout rates, NCLB, charter schools, parent involvement, and so on. Remember that paper you wrote in your Foundations class? Chances are you researched a key issue that is of national concern. You don't have to be an expert on it; just be aware of the issue and be conversational.

MISTAKE #9

Negative Body Language and Lack of Eye Contact

Resolve to ask someone who will tell you the truth about your ability to introduce yourself and carry on a conversation with comfortable body language and consistent eye contact. If you feel any discomfort with this interpersonal skill, work on it. It's really important for your success.

MISTAKE #10

Poor Interpersonal Skills

Resolve to observe yourself to see how you interact with others in different situations. Are you using communication skills effectively? This includes your tone of voice, your active listening abilities, how you approach someone with a question or topic, and how you respond to that person. If you find that you interrupt others or initiate conflict or unease in a conversation, work hard to make small changes immediately.

MISTAKE #11

Inappropriate Dress

Resolve to put on your interview outfit and go to a reputable clothing store and simply ask: "Is this an appropriate suit for an interview?" *Suit is the key word here.* Suits can be dressed down—take off the jacket and you have an entirely new look. Employers see way too many applicants dressed for a night on the town rather than a serious meeting.

OK, so back to getting those interview skills of steel in just 10 minutes a day. You might be asking yourself, is it possible? Absolutely. All you have to do is devote 10 minutes a day to tackling one aspect of the interview. Take 10 minutes to figure out your interview uniform. Spend 10 minutes a day reviewing schools on your list of 10 (remember that short list of your 10 dream teaching jobs?), or practicing your handshake. Give 10 minutes to polishing up your shoes, your smile, your fingernails. Seriously, 10 minutes a day of focused interview preparation adds up over the course of a semester to be one powerful interview workout.

BEFORE YOU GO TO THE INTERVIEW

OK, just a couple more minutes on this important topic of getting ready for the interview. The following checklist is really important. Why? When you are student teaching and preparing to interview off-campus, it's hard to remember everything. This checklist can provide a quick reminder. Go ahead and take a look at it and be ready to use it when you get that all-important interview invite.

TAKE 5 **AGAIN**

Time to Get Ready—Time to Get Hired

Take 5 minutes (and maybe a few more) to go through this interview preparation checklist. You'll be glad you did.

		YES	NO
GETTING READY	• Review application materials—résumé, cover letter, correspondence, application	☐	☐
	• Review school district website, including building information, curriculum, teaching staff, HR procedures, negotiated contracts, professional development opportunities	☐	☐
	• Review interview questions and topics	☐	☐
GETTING PACKED	• Do you have a portfolio to take with you and leave there if necessary? —Lesson plans —Assessment plan/example —Parent teacher communication —Teaching philosophy	☐	☐
	• Do you have copies of your résumé?	☐	☐
	• Writing utensils, pad of paper	☐	☐
	• A USB drive with your ePortfolio loaded on it	☐	☐
	• One professional bag—even better, a nice leather or black portfolio	☐	☐
	• Umbrella if it might rain	☐	☐
	• Cell phone (sound and vibrate set to off)	☐	☐
GETTING DRESSED	• Suit, ironed shirt or blouse	☐	☐
	• Accessories—tie, belt, bag, scarf	☐	☐
	• Coordinated socks, shoes	☐	☐
	• Groomed appearance (brushed teeth, trimmed/shaven facial hair, clean/polished nails)	☐	☐
	• Makeup and jewelry planned (nose ring out?)	☐	☐
	• Cologne or perfume left at home for evening events	☐	☐

		YES	NO
GETTING THERE	• Do you know how you're getting to the interview? Car, bus, subway, walk?	☐	☐
	• Do you know where you're going?	☐	☐
	• Do you have gas in your car? Are you aware of the traffic at the time of the interview? Arriving too early is better than arriving too late because of traffic. Pad your travel time, but if you get there too early, drive around the block and review your interview questions. Stop by the men's room or the women's room before checking in and make sure you look fresh after the drive.	☐	☐
	• Do you know where to park? Do you have a picture ID with you? You might need to prove your identity to get in the door—security is up at schools nationwide.	☐	☐
GETTING INTRODUCED	• Have you practiced your handshake and smile?	☐	☐
	• Are you ready to meet new people?	☐	☐
	• Do you know what you will say to introduce yourself?	☐	☐
	• Do you have small talk at the tip of your tongue?	☐	☐
GETTING GRILLED	• Prepared interview questions	☐	☐
	• Incorporate student centered standards-based details	☐	☐
	• Behavior-based responses	☐	☐
	• Complimentary statements	☐	☐
	• Detailed examples	☐	☐
	• Questions for them (3)	☐	☐
	• Prepared statement of thanks	☐	☐

GETTING THE MOST OUT OF YOUR INTERVIEW!

SUMMARY

Interview Preparations

This part has been all about getting ready for the pinnacle of any job search—the interview. We've walked you through various types of interviews, and the best way to prepare for each, and given you proven tips to make a great visual first impression by dressing for success. The more prepared you are for an interview, the more it shows—and, trust us, employers are watching. Make sure you're the best-prepared candidate. The following activities can help.

ON THE WEB

ePlanner Activities

1. *My Research about the Job:* What I know, what I need to know.
2. *My Job Seeking References:* Folks whom I can use during the job search.
3. *Interview Dates and Details:* Know the details, get hired.
4. *My Weekly Summary:* Keeping it real in the final stretch.

eResources

As you prepare to interview for your first teaching job, it's important to have as much information as you can about the district, community, and state. Look up the district online and find out as much as you can; visit the state Department of Education map page to find state-specific employment information, information on licensure, and even state-wide job banks.

Video Tips

The Interview—An Employer's Perspective: Listen in as an employer talks about your one chance to seal the deal—the interview. Your résumé may get you the interview, but you'll be the one to get you a job!

Getting Ready—Employer Advice on the Interview: A hiring official talks about the various interview skills, settings, and strategies you can use for a successful interview.

Getting Hired Video: The Interview—A Student's Perspective: A job seeker shares her stories of the ups and downs of the job search and interview process. Learn how to make connections to the interviewer and convince them you're the right one for the job.

PART 11

Interview Questions and Topics

Dr. Mario Andrade, Assistant Superintendent, talks about why your interview answers are so important: "If we choose to hire you, your job is to increase student achievement and prepare the students to be successful in life either in the work force or in higher education."

My To-Do List

1. Think about and prepare for the most common interview questions.
2. Prepare for behavior-based interview questions.
3. Formulate your answers with specific examples in mind from your student teaching.

My Project Overview

1. Take 5: Tell Me about Yourself
2. My ePlanner
   a. *Interview Cheat Sheet:* Notes to self on important topics.
   b. *My Weekly Summary:* Especially important for interview success.
3. Take 5 Again: My Questions for the Employer

Employers are basically trying to find out one thing in the interview: are you the best person to help their students succeed? With that in mind, let's talk about interview questions. You already know that you'll meet any number of interesting administrators involved in the interview process; some will make you feel very comfortable; others will undoubtedly make you feel a bit edgy. They are an unpredictable lot, and that's why it is so critical for you to be prepared for the types of questions you'll encounter.

TAKE 5

Tell Me about Yourself

For this Take 5 we want you to spend 5 minutes brainstorming your introductory spiel for employers. Why? Because this question is almost always the first question you'll be asked at an interview and it gives you complete liberty to potentially drive the focus of the remainder of the interview. Of course you'll want to include the basics that we discussed in an earlier part of the book: your passion (what excites you about teaching), your profile (academic background and related experiences—highlight those that are especially relevant), and why you're excited to be sitting in the hot seat at the interview (what you're looking forward to in that district—this one shows you've done your homework and is a bit of flattery). Ready, set, go—you have 5 minutes to brainstorm what will become a 2–3 minute spoken introduction.

It's fairly universal that school employers use a pre-determined set of questions. Why? This assures that all job seekers are asked the same questions, thus eliminating biases or other irregularities in the decision making process. Chances are you will be involved in interviews that use behavior-based interview questions. What's that? Here's the short answer to that question: A behavior-based question is one designed to probe your past behavior in similar situations. The question might be phrased something like this:

> *"Tell me about a time when you felt frustrated in student teaching." "Tell me about a lesson that failed."* Employers know that you've had similar experiences in your recent past, and by asking you these questions they are fairly certain that they will hear responses that can clue them in to behaviors you are likely to repeat.

TIPS FOR ANSWERING BEHAVIOR-BASED QUESTIONS

The most important thing to remember when answering behavior-based questions is to share the experience or the situation in a story form. Talk the employer through the following three points:

- What was the situation?
- How did you express yourself? What were your actions?
- How was the situation resolved?

Let's face it. There are only so many scenarios that can be presented to teacher candidates that are of value: family involvement, collegial relationships, lesson plans, student behavior, assessments, motivation, technology—you get the picture. Having some idea of the topics, you can get to work and practice. Sit down and answer the question like someone was sitting across from you. Talk yourself through the question by describing the situation, by talking about your actions and how you felt about them, and ultimately, how the situation was resolved. It's hard to do this for the first time in a formal—really important—interview. So, do it now. It won't take too long to get comfortable thinking about your answers in this form. You'll be surprised how quickly your personality and your passion will be evident in your responses.

Dr. Mario Andrade, Assistant Superintendent, advises job seekers to consider the following as they think about meaningful interview responses: "I listen to how job seekers talk about student success. First and foremost, I want to be sure that they are there for the students."

"Tell Me about . . ." "Describe . . ."

OK, let's make it easy and remove all the extra verbiage in interview questions and get right to the *point* of the question. Let's use two distinct interview categories: *tell me about* and *describe*. Get past the extra words and focus on the bold face—that's the main point. That's what you need to concentrate on. There are many ways to frame a question—but there are only so many answers about a particular topic or issue. You should be ready to share a meaningful response, regardless of how the question is asked.

The "tell me about" questions:

Tell me about . . .

- **yourself**
- why you **selected** education as a career
- your educational **background**
- **youth-related** experiences
- the type of **relationship** you established with _____ (students; cooperating teacher; staff; families)
- a **time when** . . .
- your **weaknesses**
- your **strengths**
- how you **assess** student **learning**
- how your **philosophy** is put into action
- your best **lesson** plan
- a **lesson** that failed

- your **teaching style**
- teaching **strategies** that are inclusive
- an **adaptation** you have made
- classroom **control**
- **transition times**
- an **assessment** strategy
- **adaptations** for _____ [underperforming or at-risk or accelerated or English-language learners (ELL) or . . .]
- **motivational strategies** used for _____ (underperforming or at-risk or accelerated or ELL or . . .)
- strategies used to **involve families** in your classroom
- a **typical period or day** in your classroom
- creating a **safe classroom**
- the most **satisfying** aspect of teaching the least satisfying
- **role** of the _____ (principal; counselor; speech therapist; behavioral therapist)
- your **Facebook page**
- the ways you address **student learning styles**
- the **books** you selected for your class
- a **recent book** you have read
- your **favorite author**
- your **current goals**; 5-year plans; 10-year plans
- your use or views of **social media** tools (MySpace, Facebook, Twitter)
- **communication tools** and strategies
- a **current topic** of interest to all educators
- your **extracurricular** talents and interests
- **Bloom's Taxonomy**
- **NCLB (No Child Left Behind)**
- your most important **accomplishments**
- your **desire** to be hired for this job
- how you will work with **poverty** issues in your classroom

Let's make this simple. **Employers listen for responses that:**

1. are **student-centered**;
2. focus on **student learning**;
3. reveal **student success**;
4. demonstrate your **commitment to all learners,** to all students.

It's that simple.

The Describe Questions

These questions may not be all that different from the "tell me about" questions, but remember the focus is on real examples from your experience, or what you believe about teaching and learning (otherwise known as your philosophy statement—see Part 9 if you've forgotten about that baby). Employers want to hear adjectives, action verbs, adverbs, prepositions . . . you get the picture. Make it come alive for the folks listening to your descriptive statements. Tell them something interesting, memorable, believable. Paint a picture in their mind—as vividly as possible—because they need something to grab onto and to remember about your interview answers. When interview teams regroup to discuss the strengths of each candidate—guess who gets the job? The person who told the best story.

Describe:

- how your **room was organized**
- how you handled a **behavior management** issue
- yourself using **five adjectives**
- how **others** would **describe** you
- how you **introduced** _____ (topic; concept) to class
- how you have created **accommodations** for _____ (special needs; ELL; talented/gifted; at-risk; truant; homeless)
- a **lesson** that did not go well
- how you **organize/plan** a unit; design a thematic unit
- how you have **integrated technology** in your lessons
- a **management issue** with a student
- how you **handled a disagreement** with a colleague
- how you **built relationships** during student teaching
- how would you **handle cyber bullying**
- a situation with an **unhappy/angry family** member
- a **situation** where you needed to use _____ (problem-solving skills; creativity; patience)
- an **ethical situation**
- a situation that **demonstrated initiative**
- **teaching strategies** you have used
- how you **integrated reading** into your subject matter
- your experiences with **cultural diversity**
- a **collaborative** experience
- **goals** and future plans
- a **great teacher**
- your **perfect** teaching **job**
- a classroom that **promotes student learning**
- the role of **parent(s)/family** in the **student's learning**
- what your **references** would say about you

- a **difficult problem** that you have addressed
- your **expectations** for this job
- why you **selected teaching** as a career
- your top **four qualities** as a teacher
- your **working style**
- your **fluency in a language** other than English
- what you **liked/disliked** about student teaching
- **why** you want to **teach here**
- **previous experiences** that qualify you for position
- how you have **celebrated student success**
- a telephone **call** made **to a parent**
- how you have used **differentiated instructional** practices

Think this list is overwhelming?
Tell me about it! (pun intended)
Take it easy, breathe, chill out.

We've been talking about all of these topics since the beginning of the book. You have, in fact, been discussing these topics from your first class in teacher education. The only difference now is that they are being phrased as a question in a different setting, and your responses have a lot riding on them—your future! It just seems that an interview makes everything a bit more difficult.

Let's look at how one administrator frames interview questions.

BEHAVIOR MANAGEMENT

"Describe a time when your skills in behavior management were put to the test. What did you learn from this experience?"

TEACHING STRATEGY

"Describe a teaching strategy that you use to connect students' prior knowledge, life experiences, and interests in your lesson."

ETHICS

"Describe a situation in which your professional ethics were tested and what you learned from this experience."

GOALS

"Describe goals you have for yourself in the next five years. What have you done within the last week as part of your plan to achieve these goals?"

By remembering that each employer has a distinct style in interview questioning, you'll be able to focus on the main topic and not the extra verbiage in the question.

❝*Get ready to talk about behavioral strategies ahead of time. I want you to tell me:*

- *How do you approach behavior—both positive and negative—in a variety of settings?*
- *What strategies work best with certain kinds of behaviors?*
- *How can you adjust instructional strategies to address behaviors in your classroom?*
- *How do you identify the strengths and areas that need improvement for each student, and what data do you use?*
- *What routines and procedures do you have in place?*
- *Is your approach proactive and positive? What reactive strategies, if any, will you employ?*

It's clear to me who is prepared to effectively manage behavior and who will likely need more support.❞

—Dr. Allison Bruhn, Professor, Parent, and Teacher

INAPPROPRIATE AND UNCOMFORTABLE INTERVIEW QUESTIONS

There are some questions you shouldn't be asked, and most employers work hard to avoid questions that do not apply to the job description. Conscientious employers and search teams are typically quite deliberate in preparing interview questions so that all questions are based on job-related criteria. They are focused on and interested in your academic qualifications, your related experiences, and your interests in helping students succeed. Most feel that your personal life is just that—your personal life. Unfortunately, in spite of federal and state guidelines for pre-employment inquiries, you just might encounter a random inappropriate inquiry. Some hiring officials or search team members may ask inappropriate questions out of ignorance or naiveté. And, it is quite possible that some inappropriate questions are raised innocently with no intent to discriminate. For example, an interviewer might think a question about your family will help you feel comfortable and make it easy for you to begin the conversation. Let's call it an ice-breaker.

You don't have to try to figure out what the interviewer has in mind. In the first place, you don't have time, and second, you have a 50 percent chance of being wrong. Rather than trying to second-guess the interviewer, it's a good idea to have thought about these inappropriate questions and to have decided how you will handle them.

The following are topics that should be red flags to you if they come up during the interview. Again, these topics might come up quite accidentally or without an agenda, but memorize this list below so that when you hear one of these topics during the interview . . . you know to proceed with caution:

- **Your native or first language or "mother tongue"**: Employers can ask you which languages you can speak. It's useful in this day and age to have a multilingual staff; however, questions about "native language," "first language," or "mother tongue" might incite bias or prejudice, or might be simply illegal in some states. Employers can ask if you are legally authorized to work in the United States, and they can ask what languages you speak. Again, watch out for the words: native language, mother tongue, and first language.

- **Your age, weight, height, or physique**: It's just against the law to ask about most of these things. Unfortunately, size, age, and height are areas where recognizable discrimination still persists. If any questions about your physique, or physical abilities should come up, so too should your red flag.

- **Affiliations**: Teachers come from all religious and spiritual walks of life. Additionally, teachers are Republicans, Democrats, Independents, Libertarians, Greens, and Socialists. It's not uncommon during casual chat for these questions to arise. Exercise caution in discussing any of your political, religious, and social affiliations.

- **Family status**: Employers are not allowed to ask questions about your marital status, nor are they allowed to ask if you have children or other dependents. Many states have even passed laws to address issues of sexual orientation during the interview process. Regardless, discrimination against some individuals on the basis of sexual orientation, gender identity, family status, and dependent status still exists. Know your rights, and stay in your comfort zone.

- **Medical history**: More and more job candidates are encountering questions that might address personal health and well-being. It is illegal for employers to ask about your medical history—so just avoid it. However, employers can ask if you're able to perform the job. Once hired, you may also be required to submit for a medical examination—but understand that your medical records are not a required piece of the application process.

Take a look at the list of common inappropriate questions:

- How old are you?
- When were you born?
- Are you a U.S. citizen?
- What state are you from?
- What's your native language?

- Are you married?
- Do you have children?
- Do you want to have children?
- Will you be moving here with a spouse?
- What does your wife/husband do?
- Have you ever been arrested?
- What's your height/weight?
- Do you go to church? Synagogue? Mosque? Temple? Sweat lodge? Yoga?
- Were you honorably discharged from the military?
- Do you have any disabilities?
- Tell us about your medical history—any illnesses, operations, or procedures that we should know about?

WHAT ARE YOUR OPTIONS?

JAMIE'S DILEMMA

Jamie was interviewing for an elementary teaching position in a small community. The interview began well, with a few minutes of small talk. Then he was asked about his marital status. This was a problem question for him. He was in the process of getting a divorce from his third wife, and he really didn't want the employer to know about his marital history.

There are several ways Jamie could handle this question. Because he felt that giving the information would work against him, he could simply say he would provide information about marital status upon employment. Another option would be to answer the question by saying, "I've been married, but I don't consider that relevant to my qualifications for the job." He might answer with a question such as "Is this information required?" Or he might simply say, "I prefer not to answer that question." If he felt more comfortable answering the question, he would only say, "I'm in the process of a divorce." Under no circumstances is he obligated to elaborate or to introduce the topic of his other wives. Sometimes a statement like this might snap employers back into reality and remind them of their professional obligations. Bottom line: it's natural to feel uncomfortable at the interview—but interview questions that deal with any of these topics are probably illegal, so don't feel uncomfortable not answering them.

> **"**In this day and age employers should be cognizant of state and federal laws regarding pre-employment questions. Candidates should know that if a question is not related to the job, it does not need to be answered. Tact and sincerity is your best approach.**"**

—Ann Feldmann, Assistant Superintendent

YOUR QUESTIONS ARE IMPORTANT, TOO

Most employers will save time at the end of the interview for your questions. This opportunity allows you to ask for clarification and also allows you to gather information that was not presented during the interview. This opportunity also works for employers. The types of questions you ask will give them insight into your commitment and professional needs.

Jeff McCanna, Director of Human Resources, advises job seekers to preplan for the end-of-the-interview. "It can be an awkward moment to be asked 'what questions do you have for me' and then for the job seeker to say 'none.' This is a negative way to end the interview and clues me in to your level of interest about the job. It's always safe to ask about parent/family involvement, professional development, student success rates, and staff collaboration."

Planning to Ask

It just takes a few minutes to think about general questions that could be asked of any recruiter or hiring official. Jot those questions down so you won't forget them. Listen carefully during the interview for information that you might want clarified or expanded upon. It's easy to say something like: "You mentioned that your building is involved in the (insert any number of acronyms from education) program. Could you tell me more about how I might be involved as a new teacher?" Planning ahead is always to your benefit. By drafting a few questions early you will be better prepared to refine them as you begin to get interview offers.

Employers do strongly recommend that you ask only those questions that are relevant to your success in the job. Topics that are always relevant include these:

- Community involvement.
- Evaluation and assessment methods for students/staff.
- Support systems for staff and for students.
- Established policies for student behavior.
- Family participation and involvement.
- Mentoring opportunities for new staff.
- Specific teaching materials/resources in your specialty.
- Standards and school benchmarks.
- Professional development opportunities.
- Participation in staff inservice training.

It's a Two-Way Street

Your questions carry just as much weight as those of the employer. Granted, you won't have as much time as the employer, but what you ask and how you ask it could be a deal breaker. The job seeker usually gets to have the last five minutes of the interview to ask questions. Ending the interview with intelligent questions can both strengthen your candidacy and the conversation.

TIP

A serious candidate will always have questions about the students, the district, the curriculum, and the community. It's all about the right fit. To find this fit, explore the community and make sure it has the right combination of what you need. Examine the school's website to identify a vision and curriculum. Is this the right place? Is this the right job for me? Can I be successful here?

TAKE 5 **AGAIN**

My Questions for the Employer

Employers expect job seekers to ask questions during the interview and, frankly, are concerned when candidates say they don't have any. If this job is important, wouldn't the potential teacher want to know about the curricula, the students, the building goals, and camaraderie among staff? And school discipline policies? There's no question about the value of asking meaningful questions—you'll become more knowledgeable about the position and will have a better feel for whether the position is a good match for you. Take 5 and frame questions that will help you (1) determine fit; (2) determine resources for student success; and (3) determine if you can make a difference.

SUMMARY

Interview Questions and Topics

The interview presents your chance to seal the deal. Too many candidates show up at the interview overconfident in their ability to talk about teaching. The best-prepared candidates, on the other hand, have taken time to meaningfully integrate their real teaching experiences, the details that demonstrate student success and learning experiences. Employers know you have a great deal to learn, but they need to see that you've really paid attention during student teaching to creating and nurturing the best conditions not only for student success, but for your own success as well. The comprehensive listing of interview questions and topics likely doesn't introduce anything that you haven't thought about or encountered over the last few semesters of your teacher preparation, but those candidates who have taken the time to recall and reflect on specific details, events, and the "for instance" of a given topic will be the ones who truly impress. Take some time to discover, remember, and prepare to give a "for instance" of your own. These activities will help.

ON THE WEB

ePlanner Activities

1. *Interview Cheat Sheet:* Notes to self on important topics.
2. *My Weekly Summary:* Especially important for interview success.

Video Tips

Watch three job seekers give powerful answers to the toughest interview questions. You'll learn how to give student-centered answers based on your unique experiences.

Elementary Video
Middle/Junior High Video
High School Video

PART 12

After the Interview

Jeff McCanna, Human Resources Director, tells candidates that the face-to-face interview is only part of the interview. "There is still work the hiring official needs to do. It's not over for the interviewee, either. Reflect and see if you want the job if offered; reorganize and move on if you don't get the job."

My To-Do List

1. Interview follow-up: thank-yous, and your own interview recap.
2. Have a rejection plan—be prepared with backups, and strategies to move on.
3. Determine your personal and professional fit factors.

My Project Overview

1. Take 5: My Dream Job Revisited
2. My ePlanner
   a. *The Fit Chart:* Post Interview: Deciding on school, community, life.
   b. *Personal Budget Planner:* Welcome to life after college: Survival 101.
   c. *My Weekly Summary:* One more isn't going to hurt.
3. Take 5 Again: My Dream Life

It ends with a handshake. One last handshake to permanently seal the deal. Behind the smile and handshake you're thinking:

> *Come on, you guys, can't we save both of us the time and hassle—just tell me: Did I get it, did I nail the interview? My answer to that question about classroom management was kind of weak, but I could tell I really impressed you when I talked about parental involvement and my motivational strategies. Look, I know I can do this. I really want to work here; please give me the job. I will be the best teacher you've ever seen. Besides, I bet none of the other candidates looked as good as me. I made great eye contact with everyone and it seemed to end on a positive note. Hmmm, I wonder what they meant when they said they had two other people to interview? Were they trying to tell me that although I hit a grand slam, they have to go through the formality of interviewing the other two losers? Or wait, maybe they're sending me another message, like, "Sorry, pal, we want you to know that you shouldn't get your hopes up because we still have two others to interview and we're pretty certain they're going to do better than you . . . in fact that's why we scheduled you first, to get the worst one out of the way." You turn*

and walk out the door. Don't forget to stop on your way home to pick up the Rolaids® . . . you're gonna need them.

Are you the kind of person whose glass is half empty or half full? Your answer to that question might determine how much you perseverate on the strengths and weaknesses of your interview. First off—congratulations! Trust us—nobody in their right mind would waste their time interviewing someone who didn't at least have a chance to get the job. If you made it to the interview you should feel good that something is working—either your paper materials or networking strategies, or both. Secondly, like a good cheese, you will only get better over time. The more you practice interviewing, the better you'll be.

Post-Interview Checklist

The interview doesn't end when you walk out the door. Sure, it's time to head home, but make sure that when you stop at the store to get those antacid tablets you also pick up a thank you card to send to the employer—in fact, buy a package of them. You'll probably need them. Get a thank you note in the mail right away—don't hesitate—even a day. Why? The employer might be making a decision sooner than you think, and your thank you could be the final game changer if they're deliberating between you and another candidate. A quick note of thanks—even if it's in an email—communicates professionalism and a sincere interest in the employer and the job. Make sure you thank them for the opportunity to interview and for their consideration. If something particularly humorous or endearing occurred during the interview be sure to mention that as well. Remember that part about building relationships? A quick note of thanks with a bit of personal flair does just that.

Very few candidates are offered a job on the spot—so don't celebrate yet. It's time to think about what happened and to make a few notes for yourself. Post-interview reflection is really very critical for interview success. Immediately after an interview, it's easy to remember how you answered a question . . . or the hesitation you felt when a particular topic was presented by a hiring official. These raw emotions don't last long, so capitalize on time and place and jot them down now.

Replay . . . Replay

You'll probably never leave any interview perfectly satisfied with your performance. It's always possible to think of a more sophisticated response, a different answer, a smoother exit. Hindsight is always better, but you can't back up and go through the whole process again. The best you can do is take a quick but serious look at what happened so that you can make your next interview a little sharper, a little better.

Maybe start with something that didn't go as well as you expected. If you had trouble with a response to a specific question, figure out the answer so that you'll be ready for it next time. Perhaps you need to refer to an old textbook, or call your cooperating teacher, or pull up an artifact from your portfolio to figure out a better answer. If you think you talked too much—or too little—resolve to either eliminate the fluff or add some substance. If you think you were too passive, figure out how you can show your real enthusiasm, your real passion.

Your review of the interview should help you to improve where you can, but don't let it keep you from getting on with your job search. Use your energy to pursue other jobs, not to replay old interviews in slow motion. Certainly, like some cheeses, you can reach a point where you're overly ripe—that's when it's time to begin reevaluating something in the equation. If you're getting interviews, but not jobs, maybe you need to be better prepared for the interview. If you're not getting interviews, maybe you need to take another look at the résumé (and that part of this book!), but before you tear too much hair out, understand one thing—rejection happens. It's a perfectly normal part of the job search, especially for new teachers.

Timing after the Interview

A few chapters ago we talked about timing. In that chapter we talked about the importance of wait time and patience. Understand that the interview process sometimes takes a week or two before all qualified candidates are able to interview. That means that if they're interviewing three candidates, they have to do everything in threes. Do you know how difficult it is to get search committees together three times? It can take a while, so be patient. If you've already interviewed, we feel two weeks is a good amount of time to wait before making some sort of contact with the school district or head of hiring about the status of the search. Be prepared for anything from "We're still interviewing," to "Sorry, the position has been filled." Make sure you're ready to respond to any of those statements with professional demeanor.

INTERVIEW FOLLOW-UP

It's OK to contact a school district and follow-up on the interview. A quick phone call may help you find the answer you are hoping to get.

Making a phone call—it's as easy as this:
Rings . . . School staff answers:

Job seeker/interviewee:
Hello, I'm _____ and interviewed with Dr. Jones and the committee for the _____ teaching opening on _____ (date).

- I'm wondering about the status of that position? Has a decision been made? Depending on the answer you might say:
  - If no decision has been made, can you tell me when you think the team will reach a decision? Or . . .
  - Thank you for sharing this information with me. I'm sorry to hear that I was not selected but please keep me in mind if another opening should arise.

Always thank the staff for the information and the time shared with you. An act of courtesy is never forgotten.

If you're like most candidates looking for a first teaching job, there's a good chance you'll have more than one interview. Following an interview there are typically three things that may happen: rejection, an invitation for more interviews, or an offer. We're going to take a minute to address all three.

REJECTION

Rejection never feels good. Someday, you may look back and thank the person who rejected you. Why? Because the job just wasn't the best fit for you. You didn't realize it at the time, but the hiring official did. And, you can thank the employer for knowing that. As we mentioned earlier, the biggest reason for teacher drop-out is not finding the right fit—or the right job. MOVE ON! Take a day and mope around—it's OK. Teaching is important to you and you want to be employed. After 24 hours it has to be game on again. Candidates often take rejection as a personal attack. Hey, employers don't know you well enough to get personal. They have decided that some other candidate fits the position better—maybe because that person has more experience, more education, more skills, or even more personality. You'll never really know and that's why we suggest moving on and getting the job search back in gear.

Should you contact the employer and ask why you were not selected? NO, no, and no. Employers don't like rejecting people in the first place, and they sure don't like damaging your ego any more than they already have. Occasionally, you might hear that someone is willing to give feedback after the interview. Some might call that honest, but we think it's sadistic. Trust us—don't do any more damage to your ego . . . and seriously, if you replay the interview in your mind, you can probably determine what you need to improve on your own. So, again, move on. Obviously you had the right stuff to make the short list this time and it will happen again.

> 66We've all been rejected. That's part of the process. When you get the call, be courteous and let the employer know that should other positions open up, you would certainly like to be considered. Always, thank the employer for their time and consideration.99

—Ann Feldmann, Assistant Superintendent

Employers want the best teachers to be in classrooms. It's not unusual for employers who have not selected you, but who thought you were an excellent candidate, to share your name with another district. Don't be surprised if you get a call saying that an administrator recommended you to them. Never burn bridges because of a rejection notification.

THE SECOND INTERVIEW—THE CALLBACK

Getting called back for a second interview is a little bit like a Supreme Court nominee advancing from the House of Representatives to the Senate. It's high stakes—you've passed the first round of confirmation hearings but are now usually scheduled to meet with people one step higher in the process. Second—or even third—interviews aren't common everywhere, but they aren't all that uncommon either. For some, the first interview may have occurred at a job fair or on-campus recruiting event. Your second interview may be with the building or district administrator. Some of you will be invited back for a day of interviews in which you might meet with a principal, teaching team, or district staff. Before you head out to the second interview, make sure you know who will be there and what will be expected. You're in the final running, so take any and every opportunity to polish, perfect, and inform yourself about what to expect. Serious preparation before a second or any callback interview is what will seal the deal.

THE OFFER

It most often comes as a phone call from the building principal. *We'd like to offer you the position . . . will you accept?*

Most of you will do one of two things:

1. Blurt out **YES!** before the principal finishes the sentence.
2. Drop the phone, scramble to pick it up, and then hope that they haven't rescinded the offer before blurting out **YES!**

We know that we can't really stop you from saying yes—in fact we think most of you probably should say **YES!** But before you say yes, you can feel empowered to ask a few questions—to know the details of your employment.

You might say:

> *I'm flattered by your offer and as you know I'm eager to work in your district. I have a few questions about the terms of my employment before I accept. Can I direct my questions to you or to the Human Resources Office?*

Or, what if you still have another interview arranged? You can do a couple of things. Accept this job and cancel the other interview, or ask for more time to stall:

> *I'm extremely excited about this news. May I have some time to consider?*

You don't necessarily have to go into the details of your stalling, but you can be honest:

> *I'm excited about working in your district. Your offer presents a wonderful professional opportunity. I have another interview that I'd like to honor. May I have some time to consider my options?*

It's a lot of words for sure, and we don't think you need to memorize or read from this book like it's a script; we just hope you get the general idea. It's always good to thank an employer and to be completely honest. Again, remember the importance of a good impression even after being offered the job.

Depending on the contract and where the district is with negotiations, and so on, you may not have all the answers or salary information to the penny, but you will be able to get a much clearer picture of that information. Be careful about the image you portray. Teacher unions negotiate salaries, although there are a few districts where 1:1 negotiations occur. Salary is generally a non-negotiable. You should know roughly going into an interview what your salary might be. If you teach in a high needs area or subject matter, you might inquire about supplemental pay or differential pay, especially if you've had more than one interview and are waiting to hear back from the other school(s).

If, after you make that statement, you hear something about the contract isn't yet available, or details of the negotiations aren't yet ironed out, don't think that anything suspicious is going on. Teacher contracts and negotiations can be complicated and take a while.

To Accept or Not Accept

When the time comes to accept a job there are a number of considerations that can influence your selection. In our surveys of factors influencing job choice, newly hired teachers indicate that factors like good professional fit, proximity to family/significant others, working environment, compensation, and community size played important roles in helping them make employment decisions. Indeed, as you begin to consider various schools and districts for employment, you'll likely have many questions, especially if you're applying in an area that's new and unfamiliar. Even if you're sticking close to your roots—either your placement site, or your hometown—there are still a number of variables and decisions to make. Be deliberate. Be thoughtful.

It's important that you do your homework to learn as much as you can about various districts as you apply, interview and, of course, accept employment. The amount of information that districts make readily accessible about employment is varied. Some districts recognize the power of the web to recruit qualified candidates. Some districts just can't afford a professional web designer so they do what they can. Your research will not only yield better decision-making on your part when it comes time to accept a job offer, but it also informs your entire application and interview process. Where one district might have a higher starting salary, another district might have an excellent tuition reimbursement program. We're in the midst of many transformations in public schooling—transformations that affect not only students, but also their teachers. From job responsibilities to benefits, understanding the differences can help you find the best fit.

MASTERING CONTRACTS: BEFORE YOU SIGN THE DOTTED LINE

A contract is basically a long job description. Contracts are negotiated between the teacher's union/professional association and the district. Contracts establish the employee/employer relationship and spell out responsibilities, expectations, and employment details. Most are freely available on the web. It is a good idea to familiarize yourself with the contract to learn more about the details of a job before you sign the dotted line. Master contracts are legal documents. Once signed, you have committed yourself to the legal nuances of the contract.

Some things you'll see in a contract include the following:

- School calendar
- Number of days required to work
- Hours of employment (start/finish times)
- Evaluation procedure
- Sick time/paid time off
- Student achievement/testing
- Termination processes
- Professional development expectations
- Salary schedule
- Supplemental salary schedule
- Prep time
- Deadlines

Note: As of publication date many districts/states and schools are examining alternatives to teacher pay, evaluation, and promotion. It is essential for teachers new to a district to inquire about the details of their employment with regard to these important matters. Be skillful and tactful in how you ask about such details. Remember that professionalism is what it is all about.

Some of you are willing to go anywhere. Some of you have already decided where you hope to work. Regardless of where you hope to go, look at the list of factors you should consider, or at least be aware of, as you make critical employment decisions.

TAKE 5

My Dream Job Revisited

There's a good chance you're nearing the end of your student teaching experience. You've had ups and downs, highs and lows and everything in between. Earlier in the book, we encouraged you to think about your dream teaching job. Now that you've had some serious experience in a classroom, we want you to revisit that idea again. It's not uncommon for interviewers to ask candidates what their professional needs are in a classroom. Take 5 to write about the professional qualities of a dream teaching job.

Factors Influencing Employment Decisions

Good Professional Fit

- **Mentoring/Professional Growth Opportunities**
  Does the district offer a mentoring or induction program for beginning teachers? Are there opportunities for professional growth and advancement? Does the district encourage its employees to pursue advance degrees?

- **Community Support**
  Does the school/district seem to be supported by the community, parents, area businesses?

- **Employer's Reputation**
  Does the district have a good reputation? Do colleagues speak highly of the district and its teachers and administrators?

- **Sharing of Information**
  Does the website seem professional and have easily accessible information about student data, employment, negotiated contracts?

- **Facilities**
  Are the facilities in good repair and conducive to learning? Do the schools and classrooms seem like inviting, positive, and safe spaces for learning?

Good Personal Fit

- **Cost of Living**
  Can you afford the cost of renting with/without roommates? Can you afford gas to commute? Can you afford to have, park, and drive a car?

- **Transportation**
  Can you live where you work or will you need to commute? How far? Public transportation?

- **Diversity**
  Do you want to live and work in an area that is ethnically/culturally/racially diverse?

- **Population Size**
  Are you drawn to large urban areas, or do you prefer the simple life in the country? Is suburbia forever your home?

- **Proximity to Family**
  Can you imagine going for months without seeing the parental units, or will Facebook cut it for the folks and friends?

- **Climate**
  Do you really like all four seasons, or are you ready to trade the winter boots for flip flops?

- **Recreation Opportunities**
  Can you go without the opera, live music, or the arts? What about that dream you've had of pursuing a skydiving hobby? Does the community have what you want in terms of freetime activities?

- **Safety/Personal Health**
  Does the community feel safe? Does it meet personal health needs?

TAKE 5 **AGAIN**

My Dream Life

We strongly encourage you to think of your career decisions as "whole life" decisions. That is to say that the happiest and most effective teachers are probably those who also find personal fulfillment outside of the school day, too. Some of you can't imagine living far from the mountains, others like the hustle and bustle of a large city because of the opportunities and activities available, and still others can't imagine living far from family. These are all important and valid considerations—don't pack up and go just for a job without taking a minute to answer this question: Can I be happy there when I'm not teaching? Take 5 minutes to jot down a few personal considerations that are important to you as you make your job decisions.

Does the Paycheck Fit?

- **Pay and Salary Scale**
  Does the district have a competitive salary? Are there opportunities for supplemental pay for coaching, activities sponsorship, curriculum development? Are you aware of your placement on the salary scale? (Find your degree and years of experience . . . where those two figures meet you'll find your projected salary.) Salary schedules generally don't include supplemental pay. So you might even be making more.

NEGOTIATED AGREEMENT SALARY SCALE 201x–201x

YEAR/STEP	B	B+15	B+30/M	M+15	M+30
1	39480	41460	43820	46190	49350
2	41460	43430	45800	48170	51320
3	43430	45400	47770	50140	53300
4	45400	47380	49750	52110	55270
5	47380	49350	51720	54090	57250
6	49350	51720	53690	56060	59610
7	51720	53690	56060	58430	61590
8	53690	56060	58030	60400	63960
9	56060	58030	60400	62770	65930
10	58030	60010	62380	64750	68300
11	61190	63170	65540	67900	71460
12	64350	66330	68690	71060	74620
13	64850	66830	71250	72220	76270
14	65350	67330	71900	72870	76930
15	65850	67830	72560	73530	77480
16	66350	68330	73120	74000	77940
17	66850	68830	73770	74640	78500
18	67350	69330	74270	75240	79000
19	67830	69800	74930	75800	79550
20	68330	70300	75430	76400	80150
21	68690	70870	75410	76980	80630
22	69390	71270	75910	77380	81330
23	70370	71850	76380	77750	81800
24	70670	72350	76880	78350	82300
25	72640	73830	77350	78720	82970

The first column (year/step) corresponds to the "years of teaching" a candidate has accumulated. Pre-service teaching assignments are not generally considered when calculating years of service, although some districts do consider professional experience in the content area, or related teaching experiences when placing candidates on the salary scale. The letter B refers to Bachelor's Degree and the M refers to Master's Degree. The (+15, 30) that follows refers to number of credit hours beyond the degree.

Are you able to coach, sponsor a club, chaperone an extended field trip? You may be able to apply for supplemental duties to boost your pay. Most supplemental responsibilities are paid at a percentage of the contract or have a flat rate. This information is usually spelled out in the negotiated contract.

- **Benefits Packages**
  Does the district offer medical and dental benefits at no charge to employees? Is there paid time off? Sick leave? Personal days? Are there loan forgiveness programs that might offset a lower salary? How is the district's or state's retirement program structured?

- **Schedule**
  Does the schedule seem appropriate (hours of teaching/prep time)? Teaching load, holiday/winter/break/summer breaks?

Let's be real. What's your paycheck worth? OK, so you may have grown up with delusions of grandeur encouraged by just about every television show targeted for your generation, but the fact of the matter is, your paycheck, or lack thereof, will have a big impact on your employment decision. Why? Well, when thinking about whether or not to accept employment in a district you should think about whether the future paycheck can support all this:

1. Your living expenses (rent, utilities, mortgages, groceries).
2. Your bills (student loans, car bills, credit card bills, insurance, cell phone, vet bills).
3. Your commute (gas, upkeep on the car, tolls, parking).
4. Your recreational life (eating out, movies, going out, shopping, vacationing, hobbies).

But How Do I Know How Much I Might Be Making?

It's a good idea to try to locate the district salary scale during the application process so you'll know what your salary range will be. Never ask during the interview. Then you'll need to estimate what it's going to cost you to live in the area. Will you have roommates? A commute? What about all those hobbies you hope to feed? Don't forget that in a few short months you won't be enjoying the flexible student schedule that's become an important part of your identity . . . you'll actually be working. Suddenly living next door to the shopping mall may not be as important if you're going to be spending much less time there!

Take a look at the scenario below:

Lucy Liu attended a job fair hosted by her college. Because of the excellent impression she made, she was offered follow up interviews by three districts. She interviewed with all three schools and in the meantime had done some homework about each. In one district her starting salary would be $42,000. That district happens to be in an urban area where the cost of living is relatively high. In another district the starting salary was also $42,000, but the school was located in a suburban area where the cost of living was lower. The last district she interviewed with was in a rural setting and had a starting salary of 40,000. The cost of living was considerably less than the urban district, but there were fewer options and she would need to purchase a car. Each district would present unique living needs, expenses, and challenges. Although she wouldn't need a car in the urban district, she would have nearly a 45 minute commute with public transportation based on where she'd want to live. The suburban district had more affordable and spacious housing options, but there too, she'd need a car and would have to take on a car payment. As she began to calculate the expenses and savings associated with each district, she realized that the amount she would be able to save after all her expenses was pretty negligible between the three. Bottom line—be careful about the assumptions you make with regard to salary—be sure to carefully analyze your projected income, expenses, and needs.

SALARY AND COST OF LIVING COMPARISON	DISTRICT A URBAN	DISTRICT B SUBURBAN	DISTRICT C SMALL TOWN
Salary	45,000/year	42,000/year	40,000/year
Month (after tax, SS, union, retirement)	2600.00	2200.00	2000.00
1 bedroom apartment rent and utilities	1500.00/month	980.00/month	800.00/month
Commute time to work	45 minutes (subway/bus) 120.00/month	20 minutes (gas, parking, etc.) 160.00/month	10 minutes (walk) FREE!!!
Base after housing and transportation	980.00	1060.00	1200.00

Sure, there are differences in cost, but then again there are trade-offs and benefits in all three locations. The cost of living in an urban area is generally higher than in a rural or small town setting, but some can't imagine trading Macy's for WalMart or the club scene for barn dances. Only you know where you want to live. Be prepared for the sacrifices and pleasures promised in each locale. As you interview and finally accept an offer, make sure you're taking care to inventory all your professional and personal needs. You have a life off the clock, too!

Congratulations

Accepting your first teaching job brings a considerable amount of closure to your preparation as a teacher. It's the ultimate confirmation that you can do this. Your first job represents hundreds—even thousands—of hours of hard work and perseverance. You're about to join one of the most noble professions. The excitement and anticipation of the start of the school year is likely accompanied by the relief of a job search that's concluded. Although your job search is over, you still have plenty to do before the start of the school year. Make sure you're aware of what's required of you to finalize employment terms. School districts always need to see a valid teaching license and a completed transcript. If you're applying for licensure out of state, make sure you expediently attend to your paperwork—the licensure process can be lengthy, and your district will want you to be on top of it.

Remember that package of thank-you cards you bought? If you still have a few left, it's a good idea to think about and thank everyone who got you to where you are today. Your cooperating teachers, supervisors, principal, parents, mentors have all played an important role in the process. As a relationship builder your acknowledgement of their contribution to your success is necessary—chances are you'll need to lean on them again sometime.

At the beginning of this book we talked to you about the 10 truths of student teaching. Being a hard worker, building relationships, learning from your mistakes—you remember, right? Guess what? Those 10 truths are also true for new teachers. The 10 truths are the stuff of good teachers—now go and teach. You're ready. You're there. You're hired.

SUMMARY

After the Interview

You've made it. You're near the end of student teaching. Some of you have a contract in hand, and some of you are nearing that goal. All of you deserve a big congratulations! Teaching isn't easy, and as you've probably learned this semester, you're just at the beginning of a long learning process. The classroom is a complex environment and requires that teachers use their skills and talents in the service of their passion to encourage students to strive to be the best that they can be. It's time to wrap up your learning for this semester and begin to look ahead to the next great chapter in your life. The book ends here, but your story is just beginning.

ON THE WEB

ePlanner Activities

1. *The Fit Chart:* Post Interview: Deciding on school, community, life.
2. *Personal Budget Planner:* Welcome to life after college: Survival 101.
3. *My Weekly Summary:* One more isn't going to hurt.

eResources

1. Relocation tools online
2. US Chamber of Commerce Directory
3. Realtor.com
4. Google Maps
5. National Education Association
6. American Federation of Teachers
7. Teacher Magazine & Education Week